Water quality
surveillance

– a practical guide

Water quality surveillance

– a practical guide

Guy Howard

Practical Action Publishing
Rugby, Warwickshire, UK
www.practicalactionpublishing.org

First published in 2002
Reprinted in 2018, 2021

ISBN 978-1-84380-003-3

Howard, A.G. (2002) *Water Quality Surveillance: A practical guide* WEDC,
Loughborough University, UK.

A catalogue record for this book is available from the British Library.

Since 1974, Practical Action Publishing has published and disseminated books and
information in support of international development work throughout the world.
Practical Action Publishing
(formerly ITDG Publishing) is a trading name of Intermediate Technology Publications
Ltd
(Company Reg. No. 1159018), the wholly owned publishing company of Intermediate
Technology Development Group Ltd (working name Practical Action). Practical Action
Publishing trades only in support of its parent charity objectives and any profits are
covenanted back to Practical Action (Charity Reg. No. 247257, Group VAT Registration
No. 880 9924 76).

WEDC (The Water, Engineering and Development Centre) at Loughborough University
in the UK is one of the world's leading institutions concerned with education, training,
research and consultancy for the planning, provision and management of physical
infrastructure for development in low- and middle-income countries.

Reprint published by Practical Action Publishing

About the author

Guy Howard is a Programme Manager at WEDC, Loughborough University and was previously Research Fellow and Head of Overseas Projects at the Robens Centre for Public & Environmental Heath, University of Surrey. He is involved in the revision of the WHO Guidelines for Drinking-Water Quality as the Co-ordinator of the Monitoring and Asessment component of the Working Group on Protection and Control of Water Quality. He was based in Uganda for 3 years working with the Ministry of Health on the DFID Research Project (R6874) which produced many of the lessons reflected in the manual. He has undertaken long and short-term assignments in over 20 low and middle-income countries in Africa, Asia, Latin America and Central Europe, including working for ActionAid in Sierra Leone in the early 1990s. The main focus of the editor's work in the monitoring of water supplies and development of risk assessment and risk management methods in relation to environmental health.

Acknowledgements

The approaches outlined were developed by a project team working in Uganda, Bangladesh and Ghana between 1997 and 2001. Grateful thanks are due to following for their input into this research:

Paul Luyima, Assistant Commissioner for Health Services-Environmental Health Division, Ministry of Health, Kampala, Uganda
Robert Odongo, Senior Health Environmentalist, Environmental Health Division, Ministry of Health, Kampala, Uganda
Caroline Hunt, London School of Hygiene and Tropical Medicine, University of London,UK
John Lewis, Data Processing, Aberdare, UK
Joanna Teuton, Department of Psychology, Manchester University, UK

Han Heijnen, Environmental Health Advisor, World Health Organization, Dhaka, Bangladesh
Sarit Datta Gupta, Chief Engineer, Rajshahi City Corporation, Bangladesh
Gul Bahar Sarkar, Chemist, World Health Organization, Dhaka, Bangladesh,
Jonas Jabulo and colleagues, Ghana Water Company Ltd, Accra, Ghana
Wisdom Aditey, Lynda Osafo and Carrie Bell, Accra Metropolitan Environmental Health Initiative, Accra, Ghana

The cover photograph shows staff from NGOs testing the quality of water in Afghan Refugee Camps in Pakistan in 1994. Source: Guy Howard

Contents

Introduction

This manual is designed for staff that undertake routine field activities related to surveillance of drinking-water supplies in developing countries. It was developed as an output of an urban surveillance programme in Uganda but the information will also be of use in rural drinking water surveillance programmes.

Drinking water surveillance programmes usually collect a wide range of information on water supplies. These include quality of water and sanitary risk, continuity of supply, quantities of water used, cost of water and access to water supply. These different types of information require data collection at different frequencies and using different methods. The quality and continuity of supply require most frequent monitoring. Therefore collection of data on these indicators makes up the bulk of routine field activities and the majority of the material in this manual.

The manual is focused on methods of surveillance in relation to microbiological quality of water as this is of the greatest importance to health. It covers monitoring for a range of water sources and water stored within the home. However, the manual also briefly addresses specific concerns about arsenic, fluoride and nitrate. This manual is most suitable for use in surveillance programmes that utilise on-site testing kits and is geared towards the implementation of programmes that target the poor.

The purpose of the guide is to help staff undertake field activities efficiently and effectively. The success of any surveillance programme is largely determined by the performance of field activities and thus it is critical that staff receive adequate training and support to be able to perform surveillance activities well.

This guide is part of a series and has two companion volumes: a reference manual on urban drinking water surveillance; and a manual for surveillance for co-ordinators of surveillance programmes. There is also a manual for the use of computer software for sanitary risk and water quality information management and a set of training materials. For more in-depth information such as the design of sampling networks, the planning and implementing of training and information management, please consult the companion volumes.

The manual is designed to cover all the major issues in surveillance relevant to field activities. It provides a brief overview of the impacts of water on health, which then leads into a discussion on the indicators used in surveillance programmes and how often this data is collected. The manual then discusses water quality and the processes to follow when taking and analysing water samples, carrying out a sanitary inspection and the reporting of your findings to various stakeholders. The final sections of the manual are concerned with the use of surveillance data in promoting improvements in water quality and supply.

1.

Water and health

Water is essential for human existence. Without a basic amount of water to consume, the human body rapidly deteriorates and ultimately death can result from dehydration. However, most people have access to some form of water supply that is sufficient to meet basic physiological needs, although these supplies may represent risks to their health because of its quality or because there not enough water for basic hygiene.

Whilst water is a basic necessity for life, it has many impacts on health. Most impacts relate to the:

- **Water quality:** The consumption of water which is contaminated by disease-causing agents (or pathogens) or toxic chemicals can lead to health problems. These may be mild (diarrhoea for one to two days) or very severe (including fatal). They may also be short-term (called acute) or long-term (called chronic) and these affect may affect very few or very many people.

- **Water quantity:** Poor hygiene may be caused by use of inadequate volumes of water and may lead to skin and eye diseases. In addition, poor hygiene resulting from a lack of adequate water is also a key factor in the transmission of many infectious diarrhoeal diseases.

Table 1 below illustrates the types of disease that are related to water and sanitation. This does not include vector-related diseases such as malaria as these are not specifically related to water supply.

Group	Examples of diseases
Diseases which are often water-borne (caused by consumption of contaminated drinking water	Cholera Typhoid Infectious hepatitis Giardiasis Amoebiasis Dracunculiasis (guinea worm)
Diseases often associated with poor hygiene	Bacillary dysentery Enteroviral diarrhoea Paratyphoid fever Pinworm Amoebiasis Scabies Skin sepsis Lice-borne typhus Trachoma
Diseases often associated with inadequate sanitation	Ascariasis Trichuriasis Hookworm
Diseases with part of life cycle of parasite in water	Schistosomiasis

Table 1: Diseases related to water and sanitation (School of Hygiene and Tropical Medicine, various)

Very often, the risks that individuals or communities are exposed to through poor water quality or inadequate quantity of water are influenced by other factors related to water supply. In particular three other factors may influence the risk of disease - the **accessibility of water** (usually in terms of distance or time to the water source), **cost of water** and the **reliability of the supply**. Where water is far from the home, the cost of water is high or the supply is very unreliable, insufficient amounts of water may be collected or other sources of water (such as ponds) may be used which are more contaminated. Where water is not located at the home or where water supplies are unreliable, water will have to be stored in the home and this may increase the risk of contaminating the water through poor handling or storage practices.

1.1 Infectious diseases and water quality surveillance

In terms of water quality surveillance programmes based on the protection of public health, we are particularly interested in the infectious diseases that may be transmitted by pathogens. These diseases are spread by pathogens that are found in faeces, principally human faeces, and are transmitted by the faecal-oral route that is summarised below.

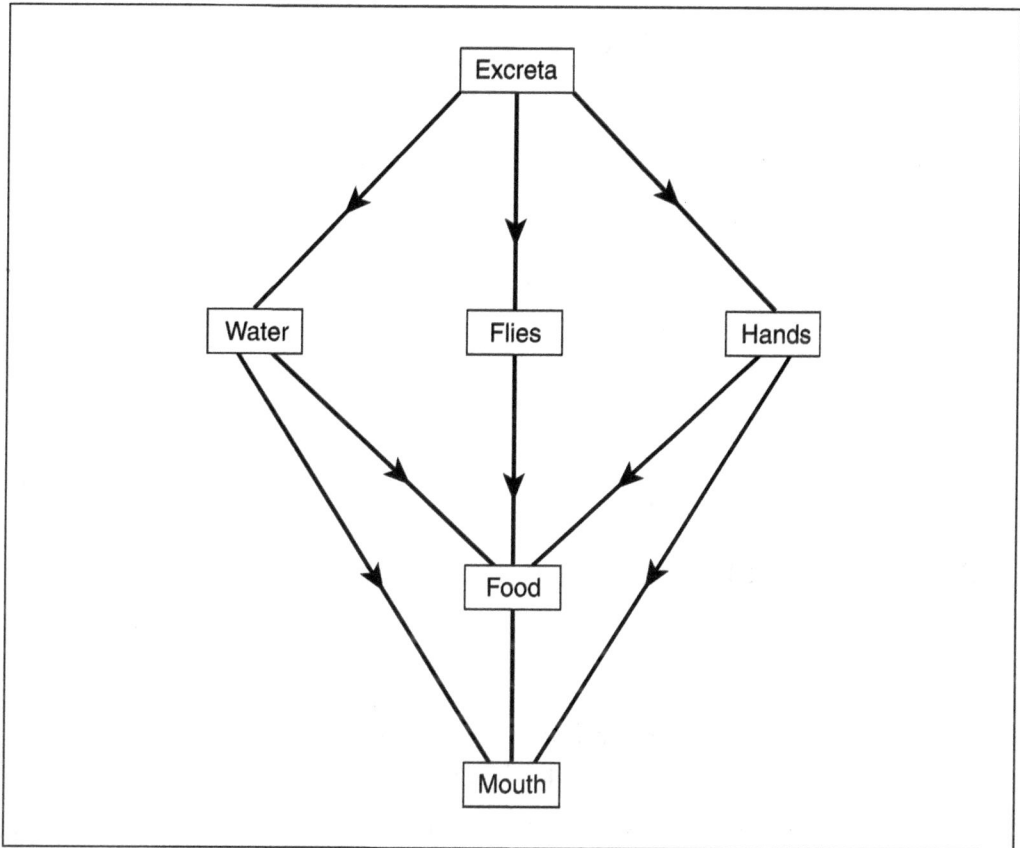

Figure 1: Principal elements of faecal - oral disease transmission

Surveillance can help break these barriers by:

1. Identifying whether faecal contamination of water sources and drinking water stored in the home has occurred

2. Identifying the ways in which faeces contaminate drinking water supplies and preventing these through source improvement and protection

3. Providing communities and households with information about their water source and drinking water and supporting them to make improvements

4. Identifying safe sources of water for drinking and cooking/food preparation and promoting the use of these sources in the community

5. Preventing entry of pathogens into drinking water by ensuring that clean and covered collection containers are used

6. Preventing the transmission of pathogens into drinking water by ensuring that people wash their hands after defecation and promoting the use of containers where water is poured and not directly scooped out

7. Ensuring that raw fruit and vegetables are washed in clean drinking water

8. Ensuring that water sold by vendors is of good quality

When surveillance programmes are implemented, a key objective is to raise awareness amongst communities about risks to their health and to identify ways to improve water sources and water handling. Thus surveillance data is used in developing technical interventions and health education as discussed later. A critical element in this process is to ensure that communities and other stakeholders have the information that can be used by them to initiate improvements.

1.2 Service quality indicators used in surveillance

There is a set of measurable service indicators that we can use to monitor and assess water supplies. These are:

1. *Quality of water* –the microbiological quality is given highest priority because of its link to infectious diarrhoeal disease

2. *Quantity of water* – the amount of water used each day by individuals and households

3. *Continuity (or reliability) of the supply* – how much of the time water is available from the water supply

4. *Cost of water* – how much people pay to obtain water services

5. *Coverage of the population* – the percentage of the population that has access to a recognisable water supply (this usually is taken to mean a supply with source protection and/or treatment)

Whilst all these indicators are important, different indicators require different types of assessment and frequency of data collection. The ways in which we collect this information and how often we assess them is summarised in Box 1 overleaf.

This box illustrates that in general, data on water quality and continuity is collected on a regular basis and this forms the bulk of routine surveillance activities. The other factors are often only assessed infrequently when inventories and water usage studies are carried out, or in the case of coverage large-scale assessments of source use, service level and compliance with accepted quality and continuity standards. In this manual we focus on water quality and sanitary inspection. If you want to know more about the other indicators, please consult the reference manual.

Box 1: Collecting information on the different indicators

Quality – this will vary significantly in a short time and over short distances. We need to consider the quality of water within the whole water chain and not simply at sources. This information is collected frequently either using on-site equipment or laboratories and is a routine activity.

Quantity – this will vary depending on whether water is available within the house, from a single tap in the yard or from a communal source. Reliability may also affect quantities used. This data is collected infrequently through a water usage study

Continuity – this may also vary significantly in a short time and over a short distance in piped water supply. Point source continuity may not vary significantly or may be due to specific breakdowns. This data will be collected frequently as a routine field activity for piped water through sanitary inspection and less frequently for point sources (e.g. boreholes, protected springs and dug wells) through inventories and water usage studies.

Cost – this may vary between sources and sometimes may change over time and in different areas. This is usually collected infrequently as part of inventories and water usage studies.

Coverage – this is often measured in terms of the numbers of people who have water supplies at different service levels (e.g. within the home, in the yard, public) and types of source. This requires large data collection exercises and is usually done infrequently.

1.3 Surveillance programme development

When developing surveillance programmes, a number of steps of followed. These are shown in Figure 2 below.

The first step will be to carry out an inventory of sources available to the population that lacks a direct household connection at a yard level or within their home. To do this, inventory forms are completed for each water source found that is available for households, which do not have a private household connection. An example form is shown in Annex 1.

In some many of the details about the source, such as the name, location and when it was constructed may already been available from records in the water supply or other offices. However, in most cases, each area be covered by the programme should be visited and the sources available recorded. This will be particularly important in urban areas where a large number of the sources may be households with a piped water connection who sell water to their neighbours. It is important to ensure that all the sources available are included in the inventory. This information is essential to develop assessment and routine monitoring programmes.

Following the inventory, a training course in surveillance techniques will be held where surveillance staff will become familiar with the equipment to be used, performing sanitary inspection and how to report and use surveillance data. The next step will be an assessment of the water in each area. This will include all the point sources that are functional, a sample of taps and a sample of households. Once this data has been collected and analysed, routine monitoring of water sources will be undertaken.

Refresher training will be usually undertaken some time after the programme has started. These may be short participatory events where staff from a number of areas come together to discuss surveillance activities and share experiences. Some times it may involve training in specific issues, such as construction techniques or health education. In some places, water usage studies may be undertaken and staff will receive training in the techniques and undertake the study. This often provides useful information for you to implement improvements in water sources and in-house water.

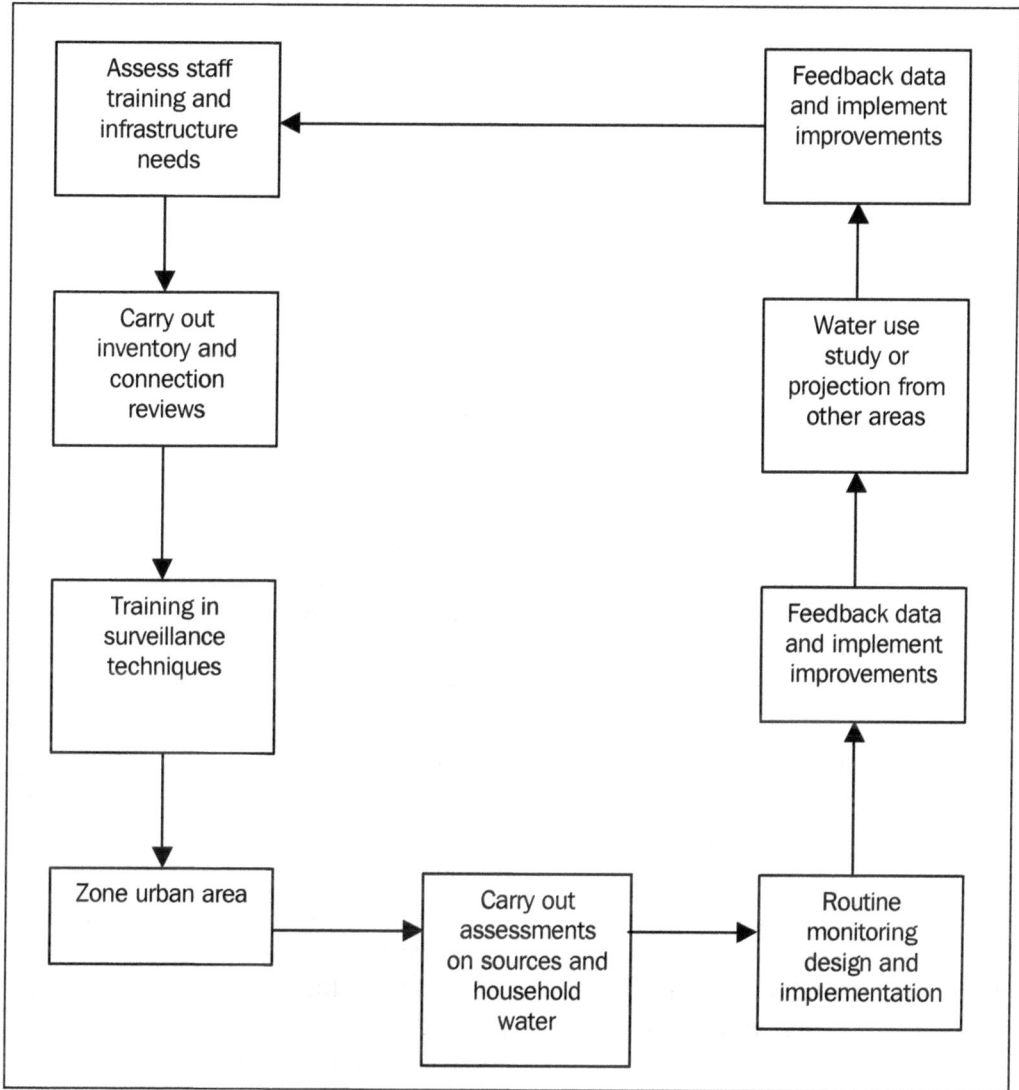

Figure 2: Surveillance development within an urban area

2.

Water quality

The primary concern with health problems caused by water supply is infectious diarrhoeal diseases transmitted by the faecal-oral route. These are caused by disease-causing micro-organisms, or pathogens. Therefore the principal concern in water quality is the microbiological quality of the water that is being consumed. Microbiological quality may change very rapidly over time and short distances and therefore requires frequent testing.

Pathogens found in water come in different forms. They may be bacteria, viruses, and protozoa. All the principal pathogens that may be transmitted by water come from human faeces and in a few cases animal faeces. Different micro-organisms survive for different amounts of time in water, have variable susceptibility to chlorine and may cause mild or severe effects. Many pathogens are readily inactivated by the action of chlorine and piped water supplies that have been treated and disinfected should have few pathogens in the final water. However, microorganisms may enter the piped water supply due to failures in the distribution network or local failures as discussed later.

Most point sources use groundwater, which in its natural state is usually of good microbiological quality. Microorganisms are removed from water by a number of processes that are grouped together under the term attenuation. These processes may lead to the permanent or temporary removal of microorganisms.

However, contamination of point sources may occur because of poor sanitary protection measures due to poor design, siting, construction or operation and maintenance. These sources also often show a seasonal variation in quality and quantity that is important for monitoring programmes.

Water may also become contaminated as people collect it from a source and take it home. This may result from many factors, such as poor cleanliness of the container, poor personal hygiene and poor storage practices. Testing this water is therefore important and the data can be used to inform health education programmes.

Parameters of water quality such as colour, odour or taste are also important. These may cause people to reject a water supply of little microbiological risk and consume water from a more contaminated supply. These are usually called aesthetic parameters. The chemical quality of water is of lower priority as in general the effects on health are long-term (i.e. chronic). There are some exceptions to this, for instance arsenic, nitrate and fluoride may all provide short-term health effects and in some cases these should be included in surveillance programmes. It is desirable that before new supplies are commissioned, a full chemical analysis is carried out to identify any significant toxic chemicals that may be present at levels that represent a risk to health. Certain chemicals may then be periodically tested on an ongoing basis. However, it is usually better to ensure that routine testing of microbiological quality and aesthetic parameters is being conducted before embarking on a routine chemical testing programme.

2.1 Microbiological quality

There are very many different pathogens that may be found in water. It is not feasible to test for pathogens directly, as it is difficult to predict whether they will be present and in what numbers. Furthermore, for many of the pathogens analytical techniques either do not exist or are expensive and time-consuming. This means that the actions required to remove or prevent pathogen entry into the water supply cannot be taken as quickly as is required and the household consuming the water are put at risk.

As most pathogens are derived from faeces, the approach adopted by most surveillance bodies world-wide to analyse the water for bacteria that show faecal contamination has occurred. These are called *indicator bacteria*. By using indicator bacteria, the number of micro-organisms that are tested for are reduced, which reduces costs whilst retaining good means to assess whether water represents a risk to health of the users. The characteristics of an ideal indicator bacteria are summarised in Box 2 below.

The indicator bacteria that most surveillance bodies use in routine assessment of the risk of faecal contamination is *Escherichia coli* (*E.coli*) or as an alternative, thermotolerant coliforms. *E.coli* provides the closest match to the criteria for an ideal indicator, however it is not perfect and it is possible to find pathogens in drinking-water supplies when *E.coli* is absent. In particular, *E.coli* and thermotolerant coliforms may not provide a good indication of the presence of protozoa or viruses. However, in general, these indicator bacteria at present provide a reasonably reliable indication of the risk of disease from the water supply. However, given the weaknesses in these indicators, water that has no *E.coli* or thermotolerant coliforms should be seen as *low risk*, rather than as *safe*.

Other indicator bacteria are also sometimes used and most common of these are the total coliforms. This is the group of bacteria that include *E.coli*, but also other bacteria that come from environmental sources and so their presence does not necessarily indicate a risk to health. There are other indicators, such as faecal streptococci and bacteriophages that may be used by some water suppliers and surveillance agencies, but are not discussed as their use is not currently widespread.

2.1.1 Other water quality parameters

Relying on *E.coli* or thermotolerant coliforms alone is not adequate to describe microbiological quality and other measures are needed. Some of these involve other analytical parameters that provide a good indication of the likelihood of microbiological quality. When combined with analysis of *E.coli* or thermotolerant (faecal) coliform, these are called the 'critical parameters'. The other critical parameters are:

- Turbidity – this is a measure of the suspended solids in the water. Turbidity is important because bacteria are often found attached to suspended particles in the water. In chlorinated supplies, raised turbidity may reduce the effectiveness of disinfection.

- Disinfectant residual – this is only relevant in supplies that have been disinfected before the water is supplied to consumers. In most water supplies this will be done using chlorine. When chlorine is added to drinking water, some is used to inactivate micro-organisms and some in reactions with organic and inorganic substances in water. In most cases, a small amount of unreacted chlorine is left in the water to act as a safeguard against contamination entering the supply during distribution. This is called the free chlorine residual and this should be routinely monitored. Another chlorine residual that may be monitored is the total chlorine level, this is the concentration of chlorine that was dosed.

- The pH of the water – this is critical for effective chlorination. Where the pH is too high, chlorine will be consumed in reactions to restore the pH back to neutral. In general, the optimum range of pH for chlorination is 6.5-8.5.

All the critical parameters require frequent and routine monitoring.

In addition to the critical parameters, other tools are required in order to ensure that the risk of microbiological quality is kept as low as possible. These include:

1. Sanitary inspection – an assessment of the hazards and contaminant pathways into the source that may cause microbiological contamination to occur. Sanitary inspections focus on the source and the immediate surroundings. Sanitary inspections are discussed later in this manual.

2. Source protection – the measures that are put in place to protect the source of water from becoming contaminated. These cover both groundwater and surface water and may include a range of measures from those in the immediate area of the source to broader protection measures.

3. Minimum treatment requirements – these will generally only cover surface water and groundwater that supplies a piped distribution network. All surface waters should be treated and this should be through a number of stages – this is called the multiple barrier principle. Where groundwater is used to supply piped distribution networks, disinfection is required.

2.2 Sanitary inspection

Sanitary inspections are a form of risk assessment and is designed to evaluate the water supply to see whether there is a likelihood of contamination occurring. Sanitary inspection data often allow conclusions to be drawn about the ongoing status of the supply and the potential risks of contamination in the longer-term. Sanitary inspection data will also identifies what interventions are required. It is a tool that can be used by community members to be able to monitor their water supply.

In a sanitary inspection, the major risks are identified that may lead to contamination of a water supply. It also provides a system that allows risks to be quantified, which is useful when limited resources mean that priorities must be set for remedial and preventative actions. There are three main types of risk factors that are included in sanitary inspections:

Hazard factors: these are factors from which contamination may be derived and are a measure of sources of faeces in the environment. Examples include pit latrines, sewers, solid waste dumps and animal husbandry.

Pathway factors: these are factors that allow microbiological contamination to enter the water supply, but do not provide the faecal matter directly. Pathways are often critical to whether contamination occurs as the presence of a hazard may not directly correlate with contamination if no pathway exists for the contamination to reach the water supply. Examples of pathway factors include leaking pipes, eroded catchment areas and damaged protection works.

Indirect factors: these are factors that enhance the development of pathway factors, but do not either directly allow water into the source nor are a source of faeces. Examples include lack of fencing or faulty surface water diversion drainage.

These factors can be incorporated into the sanitary inspection forms that are provided in Annex 3 at the end of this manual.

The sanitary inspection forms in Annex 3 have a series of questions that all have a YES/NO answer. For every question that has a 'Yes' answer one point is allocated and for every 'No' answer zero points are allocated. By summing all 'Yes' scores a final sanitary risk score is obtained. This provides the overall assessment of the source.

2.2.1 Filling in the form

It is crucial to fully understand what each question is asking when completing a sanitary inspection form for a water supply. Bear in mind that the questions are phrased so that a YES answer means that a risk is present. Therefore study the forms and questions carefully. The forms are usually reasonably simple to use and training should be provided in conducting a sanitary inspection before starting surveillance activities. Two examples of how to fill in a sanitary inspection form are given below.

Type of facility: **PROTECTED SPRING**

There are 10 questions of the sanitary inspection form and these are summarised below with explanatory notes.

Qu. 1   Is the spring unprotected?

This question asks whether the source is NOT protected. Thus if the spring is an unprotected spring, the answer will be *Yes* and if it is a protected spring, the answer will be *No*. Look for any protection works present at the site.

Qu. 2   Is the masonry protecting the spring faulty?

Look for faults such as holes in the structure, or the top breaking up. If you find any of these, the answer is *Yes*.

Qu. 3   Is the backfill area behind the retaining wall or spring box eroded?

Look for channels developing in the area immediately behind the retaining wall/spring box, a loss of vegetation immediately behind the retaining wall/spring box leaving bare earth, pits or holes immediately behind the retaining wall/spring box or the development of footpaths immediately behind the retaining wall/spring box. If you find any of these, the answer is *Yes*.

Qu. 4   Does spilt water flood the collection area?

Look to see if spilt water floods the area where people collect the water from. If you find any of these, the answer is *Yes*.

Qu. 5 Is the fence absent or faulty?

If the fence is damaged in any way (no longer reaches full way around spring), then this represents a risk. If you find this is the case, the answer is *Yes*.

Qu. 6   Can animals have access within 10m of the spring?

This is independent of the previous question as a fence may exist but does not prevent animals from coming close to the spring and possibly entering the backfill area. If you find any of these, the answer is *Yes*.

Qu. 7   Is there a latrine within 30 and uphill of the spring?

Latrines that are downhill of the spring will be unlikely to affect the spring, the distance should be determined based on an assessment of travel time. If you find this, the answer is *Yes.*

Qu. 8   Does surface water collect uphill of the spring?

Look for pools of surface water uphill of the spring within at least a 50m radius. If you find any of these, the answer is *Yes.*

Qu. 9   Is the diversion ditch absent or non-functional?

If there is no ditch, it has filled up or it no longer reaches around the full extent of the spring, then this creates a direct route for contaminated surface water to enter the backfill area and may erode the backfill. If you find any of these, the answer is *Yes.*

Qu. 10   Are there any other source of pollution uphill of the spring (e.g. solid waste)

Where sanitation facilities are poorly developed, many people may dispose of faeces into garbage or drains and this creates a serious hazard to the water source, particularly when surface water diversion ditches are not present. If you find any of these, the answer is *Yes.*

Total Sanitary risk score = the sum of all the questions with a Yes answer.

This can be converted into a percentage by dividing the total number of yes answer by the total number of questions and then multiplying by 100. Thus 7 yes answers out of 10 questions = 7/10 or 70%.

Type of facility   PIPED WATER

This again has 10 questions with a YES or NO answer. However, the format of this inspection is somewhat different because it is designed to cover a whole area rather than a specific sampling point. The form includes six questions that relate specifically to the immediate areas around the sampling points in each area and 4 questions regarding broader supply problems. At the side of each question, there is an additional line to allow you to identify at which sample point(s) the problem was found. For the questions relating to immediate sampling points, if any tap within the area has this problem, it should be answered as YES and the sample number noted. For the supply problems this is also useful, but less important.

Qu. 1   Do any taps leak?

If any tap visited in the area leaks, then this question should be answered as *Yes.*

Qu. 2   Does surface water collect around any tapstand?
If this is found at any tap visited, it should be answered *Yes.*

Qu. 3   Is the area around any tapstand eroded?
Look for signs of water channels close to the tap. If this is found at any tap visited, it should be answered *Yes.*

Qu. 4   Are pipes exposed close to any tapstands?
Look in particular at the pipe from the supply leading directly to the tap. Do not count the riser pipe for the tap. If the pipe is exposed close to any tap visited, this should be answered *Yes.*

Qu. 5   Is human excreta on the ground within 10m of any tapstand?
If this is found at any tap visited, it should be answered *Yes.*

Qu. 6   Is there a sewer within 30m of any tapstand?
Check with the household. If this is found at any tap visited, it should be answered *Yes.*

Qu. 7   Has there been discontinuity in the last 10 days at any tapstand?
You will need to ask households within the area whether this has occurred. If this is found at any tap visited, it should be answered *Yes.*

Qu. 8   Are there signs of leaks in the mains pipes in the Parish?
As you move through the area, look for any obvious signs of leaks. These may include the sudden appearance of water along roadsides or strips of lush vegetation. Also ask households in the are if they know of any leaks in their area. If any signs or reports of leaks are found, then this should be answered *Yes.*

Qu. 9   Do the community report any pipe breaks in the last week?
Ask households within the area whether this has occurred. If any reports of pipe breaks are found, then this should be answered *Yes.*

Qu. 10   Is the main pipe exposed anywhere in the Parish?
As you move through the area, look for mains pipes that have become exposed. In particular, check along roads as this is often where mains pipes are located. Bear in mind some pipes are designed to be above ground and these would not be included as a risk. If in doubt clarify with the water supplier. If the main is exposed anywhere, this should be answered *Yes.*

Total risk score = the sum of all the questions with a Yes answer.

This can be converted into a percentage by dividing the total number of yes answer by the total number of questions and then multiplying by 100. Thus 7 yes answers out of 10 questions = 7/10 or 70%.

2.3 Routine water quality and sanitary inspection data collection

The routine activities that are undertaken in water supply surveillance focus on water quality and the risks at the supply and are done on a regular basis. Sanitary inspections provide with both a useful way of identifying what the likely cause of contamination when it is found without the need for re-testing.

Sanitary inspection data can act as a predictive tool. This means that it allows an assessment of whether contamination may occur in the future even when it is not found in the sample taken. This then allows preventative action to be taken. Sanitary inspection also acts as a good measure of operation and maintenance of the water source or supply and allows weaknesses to be identified. These can be addressed through improved operation and maintenance, health education, training and support to communities managing water supplies.

Every time a sample is taken for the analysis of water quality, it is essential that a sanitary inspection be carried out. By doing a sanitary inspection we will be able to identify immediate actions required to stop contamination and to put in preventative measures to prevent future problems.

2.3.1 Routine Water quality analysis

In the surveillance programmes covered by this manual, it is expected that tests are mainly carried out for the critical parameters using portable equipment. The appropriate manual for the specific test kit should also be read. However, where samples are taken and analysed at a laboratory, the guidance provided below is still relevant.

2.3.1.1 Before you start

Preparation is the key to field work. Unless you are properly prepared, ensuring that all the items needed to do field work are available and the kits have been prepared properly, field work will become difficult and less effective. Therefore take time to plan activities.

Before leaving for the field, ensure that the following has been done:

1. The equipment (or sample bottle if used) is sterilised

2. There sufficient dishes, pads, filters, tablets and methanol in order to be able analyse samples and sterilise the equipment in the field

3. The daily report sheet and sanitary inspection forms are ready and sufficient for the field work

4. A programme of sampling has been set, so that it is clear which sources will be visited

When taking samples, there are quite specific time limits on how long the sample can be left before analysis, which may then have implications for how long can be spent in the field. If the sample is collected in a bottle and transported back to a laboratory or office, then the sample should be stored at below 4°C and analysed within 4-6 hours.

If analysis is performed in the field used a portable test kit then the filter should be left for at least one hour before switching on the incubator to allow time for the bacteria to resuscitate. However, the filter should not be left more than four hours, as otherwise there may be interference in the growth of the bacteria. This means that there are only 3 hours available for sampling and analysis in the field.

Most water testing kits also have a maximum number of samples that can be incubated at one time – for instance 16 in the Oxfam-DelAgua kit. Bear in mind, that it may be difficult to take 16 samples within 3 hours, as this is equal to 5 samples per hour (including travel between sites). Do not try and rush the sampling in order to collect many samples within the available time, as this may lead you to make mistakes. It is better to take fewer samples whose results are reliable than many that are not.

It is often a good idea to prepare the plates used for incubating the samples before leaving for the field sites, as it is time-consuming in the field. It also means that the pads do not have to be taken into the field. If the plates are prepared before departure, prepare one or two plates more than the number of samples that it is planned to take. This will allow for any mishaps in the field.

Make sure the plates are sterile before placing the adsorbent pad inside. Plates can be sterilised by either putting them into a steam steriliser for 15 minutes or by flaming them with the **blue** flame from a lighter. If a steam steriliser is used let the plates dry before putting in the pads.

When adding the media to the pads, make sure that the media is still good. If the media looks orange or yellow or if it has yellow strands or lumps in the bottle, then the media has become contaminated and **should not be used**. If the media is cold (for instance because it has been stored in a fridge), it may have clear crystals at the bottom of the bottle. These are precipitated media and not contaminants. These crystals can be re-dissolved by holding the bottle in you hand for some minutes and gently shaking the bottle.

If the media is good, then add this to the plates holding the adsorbent pads. The pad should become fully saturated with the media and there should be a slight excess liquid in the plate to prevent the pad from drying during sampling and incubation.

The media should be stored in a cool, dark place and preferably within a fridge. If the media is stored in a fridge, it should last for up to one year. However, if it is not stored in a fridge, do not use media that is more than 6 months old.

2.3.1.2 *Sterilising the equipment before leaving for the field*
The filtration apparatus should be sterile before leaving for fieldwork ready to take the first sample. The key components to sterilise are:

1. The filtration apparatus, including the funnel and the bronze disk

2. The sample cup (for an Oxfam-DelAgua kit, this is the cup which has a hole at the top)

To sterilise this equipment, follow the procedure outlined in the kit manual. Before adding the methanol, make sure the filtration apparatus is in position 2 – where the filter funnel is attached loosely to the filtration base.

DO NOT LEAVE THE FILTER FUNNEL UNATTACHED TO THE BASE AS THIS WILL FALL INTO THE SAMPLING CUP DURING STERILISATION AND MAY BE DAMAGED. ALSO DO NOT LEAVE THE FILTER FUNNEL IN A TIGHTLY ATTACHED POSITION AS THIS WILL PREVENT STERILISATION.

Once the funnel is ready, add up to 16 drops of methanol into the bottom of sampling cup. Tilt the cup towards you and let the methanol slowly run down the side of the cup. Light the methanol and place the cup on a firm surface. Once about half the methanol has burnt away, place the filtration apparatus into the sampling cup upside down and allow the equipment five (**5**) minutes to sterilise. This can be done as you move to the first site. Some key points to remember are:

1. THE FILTRATION APPARATUS MUST REMAIN IN THE SAMPLING CUP UNTIL IT IS TO BE USED. **DO NOT PUT THE FILTRATION APPARATUS INTO THE FILTER CUP, AS THIS WILL MAKE IT UNSTERILE.**

2. **DO NOT PLACE THE HOT SAMPLE CUP ON THE INCUBATOR LID AS THIS MAY CAUSE DAMAGE.**

3. REMEMBER YOU NEED TO STERLISE THE EQUIPMENT **BEFORE** EACH SAMPLE AND NOT SIMPLY BEFORE YOU LEAVE FOR THE FIELD.

The filter cup – this is the cup on which the filtration apparatus sits – does not need to be sterile, although it should be clean.

2.3.1.3 *Sampling and analysis in the field*

At each sample point, make sure through the following steps are followed when undertaking a microbiological analysis:

1. Place the kit on a firm surface where it is easy to work.

2. Sterilise the forceps by flaming them in the blue flame of the lighter. Make sure the forceps cannot get contaminated whilst they are being used. Place the forceps into the kit lid catch with the two prongs facing upwards. If anyone touches the forceps, or the forceps are placed on any surface, they MUST be re-sterilised before picking up the filter paper.

3. Take the filtration apparatus out of the sampling cup and put it carefully onto the filter cup. Ensure that you avoid touching the inside the filter funnel as this is done. Press the filtration apparatus down firmly onto the filter cup until the 'O' ring seal is within the vacuum cup.

4. Leave the assembled filtration unit on a firm surface. DO NOT place the filtration unit on top of the incubator lid as this may cause it to become stuck. If kit is used as a work surface, use the small shelf to the side of the incubator, but take care not to spill water on the kit. It is better to use another surface for filtration.

5. If the tap is to be flames, then do this using a blue flame and make sure this covers all the outside and the inside of the tap. The advantages and disadvantages of flaming are discussed later on.

6. Take the sample cup to the source. First swill the sample cup 3 times with the water to be tested. This is important as it removes any methanol traces

that may been left in the sample cup and which may prevent the bacteria from growing. Once the cup has been swilled three times, take the sample to be analysed.

7. Put the sample on firm surface away from potential contamination and close to the filtration unit. Take a filter paper and open the packaging. Take the funnel of the filtration unit and HOLD IT. DO NOT PLACE THE FUNNEL ON ANY SURFACE AS THIS WILL MAKE IT UNSTERILE.

8. Take the filter paper and place it gently on the bronze disk, making sure that it completely covers the disk and is evenly placed.

9. Replace the funnel and tighten it into the filtration position.

10. Pour the sample water into the funnel. The funnel often has several markings equivalent to particular volumes - the most common are 100ml, 50ml and 10ml. When water is in a small container, the top of the water is not entirely flat, but has a slight U shape. This is called the meniscus. Make sure that the bottom of the meniscus is level with the graduation for the sample volume you are taking.

11. Place the vacuum pump into the small hole on the side of the filtration unit. Gently press the pump a few times to start the water flowing. It may be necessary to press the pump several times to ensure all the sample has gone through. Try not to press the pump too hard as this may make it difficult to pump again.

12. Once the sample has passed through the filter paper, disconnect the vacuum pump and loosen the filtration funnel. Take a plate from the stack and open it, leaving the top resting on the base.

13. Take the filter from the base of the filtration unit carefully with the forceps and lay the filter paper on top of the pad evenly. Make sure the paper completely covers the pad and make sure no air bubbles are present under the paper, as this will prevent any bacteria present from growing.

14. Place the lid on top of the plate and put the plate back into the stack. Make sure that the plate is marked so that you remember which plate was taken from which source.

15. Throw away the remaining sample and dry the filtration unit and sample cup. RE-STERILISE THE FILTRATION UNIT AND CUP READY FOR THE NEXT SAMPLE.

The other tests that you will carry out are simple.

For turbidity, pour water into the tubes slowly until you cannot see the black circle at the base of the tubes. If you can still see the circle when the tube is full, record this as being less than 5TU (<5TU).

Chlorine and pH will only be tested for piped water supplies or household water where chlorine has been added. First of all, swill both sides of the comparator out with water that you will test. Fill each chamber up to the top.

Add a **DPD1 tablet** to the left hand side (marked DPD) and a **phenol red** tablet to the right-hand side (marked pH). DPD1 tests for **free** chlorine residual and phenol red for **pH**. Shake the comparator well until the tablets are fully dissolved. Hold the comparator up in the light. Choose which standard colours on the side of each chamber the water with tablet matches most closely and read off the value that this colour is equivalent to. To test for **total** chlorine, add a **DPD3** tablet into the chamber marked DPD where you put the **DPD1** tablet. Make sure the **DPD1** tablet has been previously dissolved in the water as otherwise you test for **combined** chlorine.

Record your results on the daily report sheet like that shown in Annex 2 at the back of this manual. On the top of the form fill in:

- The town or District

- The area or village where have done the sampling

- The date when you took the samples

- Name of the person carrying out the sampling

For each site, mark:

- The sample number (1,2,3 etc)

- The source name

- The code number of the source (if one has been allocated)

- Whether a sanitary inspection was performed

- The sanitary risk score

- The time the sample was taken

- The colour of the sample (this is just a visual assessment, clear etc)

- The turbidity

- The free chlorine

- The total chlorine

- The volume of water filtered

At this point leave the thermotolerant coliform data as this cannot be filled in until you have incubated the samples.

2.3.1.4 *Incubating the samples*

Once you have finished you sampling, the plates must be left for at least **one (1) hour before switching on the incubator**. The samples should incubate for a minimum of 14 hours. If the kit is being run from an electricity supply, the samples can be incubated for up to 24 hours. If the battery is being used, never incubate a sample for more than **18** hours. Incubation is usually best done overnight. If the incubator is switched on at 3.00pm, switch it off the following morning around 9.00 a.m.

2.3.2 Reading the membrane filtration test results

Once the incubator is switched off, read the results immediately. The thermotolerant coliforms form yellow colonies on the MLSB media used in the Oxfam-DelAgua and many other kits. Only count the yellow colonies that are at least 2mm in diameter. DO NOT count any colonies that are clear, red or any other colour, as these are not thermotolerant coliforms. If you use a different media, for instance Maconkey broth, make sure you are clear what thermotolerant coliform colonies look like.

The filter papers have a grid on them to make counting the colonies more easy. Count the colonies systematically, counting all colonies in one column of the grid before moving to the next column. Note down the number of colonies found on the daily report sheet. Where there are so many colonies that it is impossible to see individual colonies clearly, mark the result as too numerous to count (**TNC or TNTC**).

The standards format for reporting microbiological results is the number of colony-forming units (cfu) per 100ml. If you used a 100ml sample, this is the same as the number of colonies counted. If less than 100ml is used for analysis, the number of colonies found will be multiplied by the proportion of 100ml that was used in analysis. Thus, if 50 colonies are found on a plate that came from a 50ml sample, multiply by 2 to get a figure for 100ml (this would be 100cfu/100ml). If a 10ml sample had been used, multiply by 10 (in this case you would have 500cfu/100ml). Note these on the daily report sheet and keep this safe ready for data entry.

It may be necessary to take smaller volumes for analysis for a number of reasons. Once the number of colonies on a plate exceeds 200, the validity of results may be compromised as the competition for limited nutrients from the media may have caused some bacteria to fail to form colonies or for their size to be small. Where heavy contamination is found, the colonies may start to coalesce, making identification difficult. Thus it is better to take a smaller sample so that the colonies can develop more effectively. In other cases, the water may be very turbid and thus a smaller volume is used to prevent the filter becoming clogged.

2.4 Sampling site selection and sample approaches

Selecting where we take samples from and how often samples should be taken is often critical to how useful the results from surveillance are. In order to develop effective monitoring programmes we need to take into account what may cause variations in water quality, when these variations may be seen and how many people use each type of source.

2.4.1 Point sources

For point sources, sample site selection is simple, as there is usually one well-defined outlet that is used by the population. In the case of a borehole, this will be the handpump and in the case of a protected spring this will be the outlet pipe. In other point sources, such as dug wells, samples could be taken from the handpump or windlass or directly from the well itself. The frequency of sampling of point sources will be determined by the likelihood of variation in water quality, the quality determined during the assessment and the number of people using the source.

As a minimum, we want to test point sources when the quality is likely to be worst in order to assess whether there is likely to be a risk to public health. This would usually be during periods of rainfall (the wet season) and sometimes immediately after a heavy rainstorm. Some shallow groundwater sources may show very rapid response to rainfall.

In order to evaluate overall performance of these sources, it is also useful to test them during periods when the quality will be likely to be better – i.e. during extended dry periods. This data can be used to assess whether the sources are subject to significant year-round pollution, which may indicate that contamination is more widespread and therefore improvement of the source will be difficult. Alternatively, contamination may be found just after heavy rainfall, which may indicate that this is caused by a very localised problem. In such cases control of pathways may be most important to reduce the risks of contamination. Such findings will also help target health education programmes so that they concentrate on the times of greatest risk.

The frequency of sampling may also be increased where the point sources are located in high-density areas, as the amount of faecal mater in the environment will be higher and greater numbers of people will use each source. This will increase the risk of contamination and the numbers of people potentially affected. Sampling may also be increased where the condition of infrastructure is poor, making contamination more likely. Where water usage studies have shown that many people use point source and that relatively few people use piped water, a greater frequency of point source sampling is recommended.

It is important to consider whether the outlet should be flamed before the sample is taken. This depends on what exactly you wish to test:

- the quality of water in the source, or

- the quality of water actually being collected by the users.

Flaming is usually carried out when the quality of the water in the source is being directly tested. Flaming is usually carried out to eliminate any bacteria that may be on the outlet itself, which have been introduced by the users through poor hygiene. However, it is often more useful to know exactly what quality of water is being collected by the users and therefore an unflamed sample is preferred. By taking both a flamed and an unflamed sample, an assessment can easily be made of the source of any contamination that is found. This may help direct health education programmes. Obviously the outlets of some sources cannot be flamed (for instance protected springs) as water flows continuously.

2.4.2 Piped water sampling and choosing sample sites

Piped water supplies may vary significantly within a short period of time and over a short distance. This variation is not usually caused by a defined external event – for instance the season – but due to poor control of treatment or re-contamination within the distribution network. As the variation is often less easy to predict than for point sources, more samples are required from piped water supplies than from point sources. The numbers of samples to be taken is usually based on the population that is served by piped water. This may need to be calculated based on water usage study data where multiple source types exist. The table below gives the recommended minimum number of samples to be taken from piped water supplies.

Population	Number of samples per month
Below 5,000	3 sample per month (source/treatment works, plus 2 in distribution)
5,000 – 100,000	3 samples, plus 1 extra sample per 5,000 extra population
Above 100,000	1 sample per 10,000 population plus 10 samples

Table 2: Sample numbers by population

In urban areas, it is more helpful to sub-divide the town or city into smaller areas. These may be administrative or based on the piped system characteristics such as service reservoir, age of pipes etc. Thus, rather than basing the number of samples on the total population of the town that uses piped water, this is based on the population in each area.

There are some points in the piped water supply where samples should be taken regularly. These are the final water leaving a treatment plant (or the nearest point that is accessible) and from service reservoirs/storage tanks (or the nearest tap where access is difficult). In addition, samples should be taken from the distribution network. When sampling from the distribution network, a random approach to sample site location should be used. This means that each time an area is visited, samples are taken from a different tap. This greatly increases the chances of identifying contamination events. Fixed sampling points are not appropriate and often give misleading results.

Flaming will be a major issue in piped water supplies. Flaming is of greatest use when the actual water in the system is being tested, which may be important to determine when the data is used to regulate the water supply. However, in many cases it is more important to know the actual quality of water that is being collected in order to focus health education and operation and maintenance training on maintaining a safe source.

2.4.3 Household water sampling and selecting sampling sites

Testing the water stored in households is a key routine surveillance activity. Water may be good at the source, but once it reaches the home, it may have become very contaminated due to poor handling and storage. Routine testing of household water is important to ensure that the water consumed is of good quality and where it is not, to use the surveillance information in health education to promote safe water handling.

The number of households and their location included in the monitoring programme is likely to vary depending on the objectives of the monitoring. If a routine programme of household water quality testing is undertaken, the number of samples taken each month will usually be defined based on the number of people likely to store drinking water in the home and the resources available for surveillance. In this kind of programme, the households selected for water quality testing should be varied from month to month, although like the piped water sampling areas from which samples are always taken may be defined.

In other cases, the testing may be part of a specific study that is related to a health education or other intervention. In this kind of study, an assessment of the impact of the intervention is made by comparing the water quality in the study group and the water quality in a control group that receives no intervention. This helps in deciding whether improvements in water quality in the intervention group are due to the intervention or simply chance.

2.5 Chemical tests

In some areas chemical tests apart from chlorine and pH may be needed, which will usually be carried out on point sources or sources supplying a piped network. The three chemicals of particular importance are arsenic, fluoride and nitrate. Other chemicals should be tested during source selection or periodic evaluation, unless their presence leads to rejection of water supply for instance iron and manganese, when more frequent analysis may need to be carried out.

Surveillance agencies usually only undertake very limited chemical testing, given the costs and the often stable nature of chemicals in water. However, water suppliers are likely to undertake more frequent chemical analysis and may be required to by the water law.

Nitrate

Nitrate is usually derived from human activity and may come pit latrines, organic solid waste and inorganic fertilisers. Nitrate is of concern to health because it causes methaemoglobinaemia ('blue-baby syndrome'). Nitrate is very stable in water with sufficient oxygen (for instance shallow alluvial aquifers) and concentrations will only be reduced through dilution. Therefore nitrate represents a long-term hazard to the water resource. Nitrate may show seasonal peaks and so timing of sampling is often critical. Usually increases in nitrate are found as a wet season progresses and concentrations decline during dry seasons. If sources contain raised nitrate, the long-term viability of the source is questionable and alternative sources may need to be investigated.

Analysis of nitrate is best done at a laboratory, although there are some accurate field spectrophotometers that provide reliable results. If you use photometers or probes, the results are only semi-quantitative and are probably only useful in trend monitoring.

Arsenic and fluoride

Arsenic and fluoride are often derived from natural sources where minerals bearing these substances are found in bedrock. Excess fluoride causes dental and skeletal flouorsis which is an extremely painful and debilitating illness. Arsenic is related to cancers and is of increasing concern in many countries where high levels are found in groundwater and large numbers of people are affected. Both chemicals should be tested when a source is being developed, particularly in areas where there is a suspicion that they may exist because of the underlying geology or where mining or industrial processes are known to release it into the environment.

Arsenic may require more frequent testing as it appears that concentrations may increase when abstraction of groundwater leads to changes in the sub-surface water chemistry. At present, accurate results for both chemicals can only be obtained from laboratory analyses, although some field kits are available for arsenic. When these chemicals are found in water, an alternative source should be found or if this is impossible, the water will need to be blended with water with low concentrations.

Iron and manganese

Iron and manganese cause problems with the acceptability of the water and may cause consumers to reject a water source that is otherwise of good quality. Neither iron nor manganese have an impact on health, but cause discoloration or the water, staining of clothes and sanitary ware and may impart an unpleasant taste.

Iron and manganese should be tested during source selection and subsequently tested infrequently in the source waters. Unless the distribution systems is made of iron pipes, routine sampling in distribution systems is not usually carried out, although samples may be analysed in response to consumer complaints. Testing is usually done by the water supplier rather than the surveillance agency.

For testing of other chemicals, please see the reference manual on urban water supply surveillance or WHO Guidelines Volume 3: Surveillance and control of community water supplies.

3.

Reporting the findings of surveillance

Reporting on the findings of field activities is an essential step in routine surveillance. There is little point in collecting a lot of useful information unless this is shared with the people who are responsible for design and construction of water supplies or operation and maintenance. Reports t should always be made to the communities where samples were taken. People have a right to know the quality of their drinking water and the steps that they can take to prevent diseases. In many cases, the actions required to improve the source will be the responsibility of the community themselves. Improvements in handling and storage to improve household water quality in particular need to be done by the households themselves.

Other people may also need the results and conclusions. Water suppliers will need to be made aware of problems within their water supplies so that action can be taken. The local planning authority may also need the information for planning interventions to improve water supply, to focus health education programmes and to be able to promote improvements in water supply.

The different groups of information users have different needs and the way in the findings are presented and how often reports are provided may be crucial in making sure actions are taken. In the following sections, the process of information sharing is described, but please be aware that what is most important is to find out who wants the information, how often and in what format.

3.1 Community feedback

One of the most important groups of people who need access to surveillance results are the communities where samples were taken and done sanitary inspections. Obviously, these people will want to know whether their water is safe, what risks are involved in drinking the water and what they can do to improve their water quality.

However, whilst communities need the information that is generated it would be impossible to go each member of the community and discuss the results with them. It is also important to remember that most people will have only a very limited understanding of what the information means. Therefore try and make sure the information provided to the community is in a format that they can understand. In most cases, people will want more than just information about the risks – they will also want advice about what to do to reduce the risks of contamination and how to improve their water supply or hygiene practices.

The first stage in planning a feedback mechanism to a community is to decide how to get the information to them. There are several ways in which this can be done:

1. Provide a report to a local community organisation. This could be a local council or a local development committee, NGO or community-based organisation (CBO) or perhaps a local clinic or health centre. It is important to select an organisation that has regular meetings with all the community and which is able to disseminate the findings on water quality and sanitary risk to the majority of the community.

2. Put results up in a central or commonly visited place within the community (e.g. a community centre, health centre, school, church or mosque). If this is done, make sure that community members are aware that this is the place that they can find information and make sure that the information is provided in a simple format that requires little explanation.

3. Community meetings. This is often a very good way of sharing the information with the community and has an added advantage in that wider discussion can be initiated about the meaning of the findings and what the community can do to improve their water supply and household water quality. However, although such meetings are useful, also bear in mind that these meetings may fall outside normal working hours and extra time may need to be set aside to attend them. A further point to keep in mind is that whilst community meetings are important, the community themselves will usually have many other things to discuss and may not respond well to over-frequent meetings.

Often the best way to plan feedback to the communities is to combine two of the above approaches or even all three. Thus regular feedback can be provided to a community organisation, for instance each month, with community meetings held on an occasional basis (for instance twice a year).

3.1.1 Community meetings

When holding a community meeting, you must be well prepared beforehand as otherwise it is likely that the meeting will not be useful in promoting improvements in water quality. It is essential therefore to think about what objectives are for the meeting and what kind of information is being provided and the sort of questions this may generate.

It is not a good idea to plan a community meeting solely to provide information. The community members will almost certainly want advice and possibly seek direct support. When holding a meeting, therefore, the objective should be to discuss the findings with the community in the light of initiating local action to improve the water supply.

The types of questions that are likely to be raised are: 'will we get diarrhoea from our water?', 'what can we do to improve our water supply?', 'what can you do to help us?'. Be sure these questions can be answered and try to develop a discussion about what the community can do themselves and how important they view improvement of their water supply. Use health education materials to generate a debate about what can be done by the community to improve the water supply. One good method of doing this is to take a water sample with community members the day before the meeting and read the results with the community at the meeting. Show them the plates that were incubated and explain what the colonies mean. Very often people react positively to such direct ways of reporting results and they often do not need to understand germ theory to be aware that contamination is bad for their health.

In particular, be aware that many people might expect the organisation undertaking the surveillance to make the improvements, rather than taking responsibility themselves to improve their water supply. It is essential to be clear what exactly can be offered in terms of support to the community – whether technical, financial or advocacy – and be sure that this is understood. Otherwise, people may blame the surveillance organisation for failing to improve their water supply. Key points to remember are:

1. Do not make promises that cannot be kept– explain what can and what cannot be done

2. Be positive about the things that the surveillance agency and the community can do to improve the water supply

3.1.2 How to relay the information

The way in which the information presented to the community will be important in determining how well it is received and whether communities will use the information to improve their water supply. There is no point in providing communities with information such as the number of faecal coliforms per 100ml or the total risk score as people may not understand these and a significant amount of time must be spent in explaining what these results mean.

To provide a simple report to a literate community, the forms at the end of this manual can be used. These provide basic information about the water quality and risks and identifies what the major problems are. Make sure to note the major problems that are within the power of the community to address. Where other risks are found that the community may not be able to directly address – for instance interruption in supply or latrine proximity to the source – try to provide other advice such as recommendations to use tap water for drinking, or to report faults to the water supplier.

Where communities are not literate, you can modify these forms to show the degree of contamination and the risk score in terms of colour. However, be aware that this will require more explanation to be sure that people understand what the different colours mean and what they should do about their water supply.

3.2 Informing the local planning authority

The local planning authority should be provided with reports on surveillance findings every month. This is partly to ensure that appropriate action is taken where necessary and also as a way of reporting on the activities that have undertaken. The local authority needs different information from that required by communities and the information can be more technical and detailed.

The information provided should still be in a summary form – there is little point in providing all the daily report sheets and sanitary inspections forms. The information that should be included should cover:

- The sources and areas visited each month

- How many samples and sanitary inspections have been carried out

- What were the results of the analysis and sanitary inspections

- What actions have you already taken or planned with the communities concerned

- Recommendations on other actions required

- Plan for the next period

3.3 Water suppliers

It is important to share the findings with the water supplier in the area. This is important not only when problems are found, but also when water quality is good. The process of information sharing is often a key element in developing a better co-ordinated response to poor water supply.

When reporting information to water suppliers, make sure that they receive the information that is relevant to them. The information that should be provided should relate to the samples you have taken from their water supplies and the sanitary inspections carried out. Water suppliers are not responsible for household water and unlikely to be responsible for point sources. Therefore there is little point in providing this information unless it is specifically requested.

4.

Using the surveillance data

There is little point in collecting surveillance data unless it can be used to make improvements in water supply or water handling. Sometimes, the use of the data may require other people to make decisions and therefore the surveillance data becomes a very useful tool to influence decision-makers.

The key part of this process is to make sure that the data is reliable and comprehensive. Trying to influence decision-makers who may have very limited budgets is difficult when the data provided is scanty or unreliable. As decisions made to improve water supply usually involve the commitment of substantial sums of money, it is essential that this is based on sound data.

In many cases, interventions are required at a community level, possibly to improve operation and maintenance of communal supplies or to promote safe water chains. Again, these interventions should be based on sound data and the surveillance programme should be a key component in designing and implementing community-based interventions.

4.1 How can surveillance data be used?

Surveillance data can be used to direct the improvement the water supply and water quality through a number of ways and at various levels. There are policy issues that can be influenced by surveillance data by indicating where improvements to water supplies should be prioritised, what types of improvement should be implemented and what additional needs are required to support sustainability, for instance training of community caretakers and supporting water source committees.

4.1.1 Assessing the data

The first step in planning interventions is to be sure what the information is actually indicating. There are some very simple ways that data can be assessed. For instance, differences in contamination of different sources can be assessed and the type(s) of water source(s) that are most contaminated identified. This assessment can also investigate whether the contamination is related to particular seasons. If one source type is generally more contaminated than others, this information can be used to:

1. Inform health education to emphasise the use of other safe sources in the community

2. Lobby for extension of the safe water supply to more people

3. Where the contaminated sources are heavily used, raise funds to improve these sources.

In the last case, look at the sanitary inspection data and decide whether this indicates that there is likely to be widespread contamination of the whole water body or whether contamination is localised. Localised contamination will often be seen where there is a large variation in quality between wet and dry seasons and where there are significant recording of pathway and indirect risk factors. In these cases, it may be worth trying to look at how often different risk factors were reported under different water quality result categories – for instance 1-10FC/100ml, 11-50 FC/100ml. 51-200FC/100ml.

It is important to assess the household water quality results. Often source waters are of good quality but household water highly contaminated. In this case, the focus of any intervention should be on health education around the safe water chain. In other cases, water quality in houses may be very variable and it may be worth following up to see whether the source type influences this in any way.

4.2 Engineering interventions at water sources

Engineering interventions may be needed on all kinds of water sources. These need to be considered carefully and planned to reflect the ability of the communities to maintain improvements in water supply and what is most cost-effective. The technical improvement in water should be based on the sanitary inspection and water quality data. Of particular importance is to look at the sanitary risk data and to assess what this indicates about improvements that should be made.

The deterioration in the basic sanitary protection measures shows that the water source has not been well maintained and that the community has not been able to sustain the source. It is important therefore to work with the community to find ways in which they can improve the sanitary protection. When undertaking such improvement, it is also important to ensure that other protective measures, such as fences and ditches are also improved, as these may be critical in ensuring that other parts of the source protection measures remain in good condition.

The surveillance programme should also promote improved environmental hygiene around the source, including the removal of solid wastes that are uphill and/or close to the source and the draining of stagnant surface water within the immediate area of the source. It is also important to work closely with the community to try and control the construction of pit latrines and animal enclosures close to the source.

4.2.1 Protected springs

For protected springs, it is important to look at the state of the protection works – including the backfill area – to see whether these show any deterioration. In many cases, the deterioration in the immediate sanitary protection works is more important in causing contamination than the hazards such as pit latrines. However, the deterioration in the sanitary protection measures are important to improve irrespective of what the quality of water is like from any samples taken.

For instance, the catchment area may become eroded and lose its vegetation cover and at the same time there is no fence and the uphill diversion ditch is either absent or faulty. The erosion of the catchment areas results from two major factors. The lack of a fence means that both people and animals can get access directly onto the catchment area and may cause erosion by creating footpaths or by making holes in the ground. The lack of a diversion ditch allows surface water to run directly onto the backfill area that not only causes erosion but also may allow water to directly enter the water source. If only the backfill area is improved without putting in place the fence and diversion ditch, the risk of contamination in the longer-term will remain.

In this case, the technical intervention will require three stages:

1. Improve the catchment area by laying murram and new grass

2. Build a fence

3. Build a diversion ditch – one way to do this is to use large flagstones with a mortar mix or by casting concrete.

Designs for protected springs should be used that enclose the area for where backfill media will be placed, which enables both flow to be directed towards the outlet pipes and to ensure that filtration is maximised during flow through the backfill media. This is shown in Figure 4 below. The backfill media should be gravel with a nominal diameter of less than 25mm. This provides filtration potential than larger aggregates that are often used, thus increasing the possibility of removing contaminants that may enter the structure. The gravel pack should be overlain by layers of clay and sand to provide additional protection against the entry of contaminated surface water with a top layer of soil, which is essential to be able to support an adequate vegetation cover

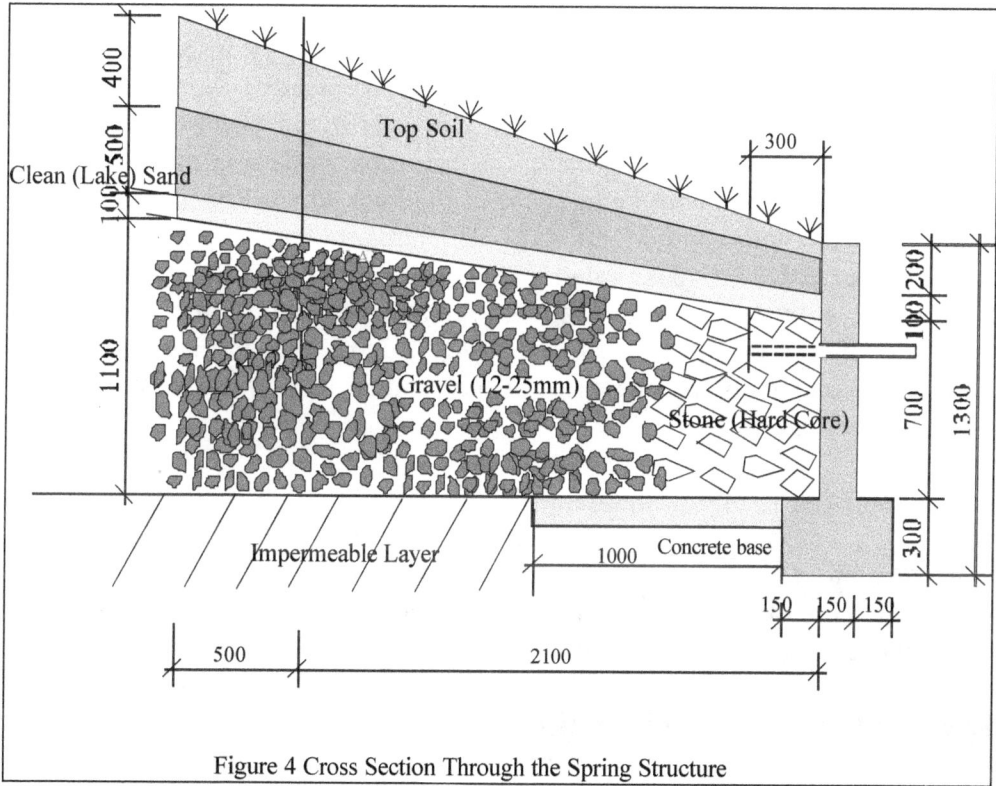

Figure 4 Cross Section Through the Spring Structure

The spring box should always be protected from erosion and inundation. This can be done by providing an uphill diversion ditch that has a concrete lining, stone pitching or well-compacted clay and putting a fence around the protected area.

The number and size of outlets of the spring should be carefully considered. In many cases, there is a problem of congestion at the source and this may lead to significant problems. This may be overcome by increasing the number of outlets by constructing a spring box with outlets on several sides. Where this is not possible, several filling points can be fitted to a single delivery pipe by using 'T'-junction. It is also usually better to use smaller diameter pipes for the outlets. When large pipes are used, a large proportion of the water may be lost during collection and this may increase problems with congestion. By using a smaller pipe diameter, not only can the water be directed more effectively into the collection vessel, but may also allow more pipes to be used.

4.2.2 Boreholes

It is often found that boreholes have a better water quality than other point sources because they are sunk deeper into the ground and often have greater protection against contamination. However, use the sanitary inspection data to identify whether any problems are noted in the protection works. This may include poor drainage of wastewater that allows stagnant water to form pools close to the borehole, the deterioration in the apron leading to undercutting of the borehole or a handpump being loose at the base where it is attached to the apron. These all require attention to prevent future problems and the community should be encouraged to make minor repairs and clean the environment close to the borehole to prevent contamination. Again, where fences are lacking and there is no means of ensuring surface water cannot flood the apron area, the risks of contamination will increase and you should work with the community to address these problems.

For boreholes, it is often important to prevent latrines and animal enclosures from being constructed close to the borehole as these may allow direct contamination of the groundwater. You should always try to ensure that such hazards are at least 10m away from the borehole and if there are latrines uphill, you should increase this if possible.

Boreholes where the top of the rising main (the pipe that comes out of the ground) cannot be sealed represent a particular hazard as this means that surface water may be able to directly enter. In this case, try to create a concrete ring around the top of the pipe and if possible seal this by making a small plinth for the handpump to rest on and extend the rising main into the base of the handpump. Where possible, try and avoid using drilling techniques that make it difficult to close off the top of the rising main.

4.2.3 Dug wells

Dug wells are often more vulnerable to contamination than other point sources because it is difficult to make the lining of the well impermeable and often the means of withdrawing water is insanitary. In some cases, dug wells are constructed to reduce the specific risk of guinea worm transmission and therefore only have an headwall to prevent people from entering the well. However, such wells may still be contaminated and it is therefore preferred that dug wells should be covered and either a handpump or windlass installed to withdraw the water. Where water is collected by a bucket, this may contaminate the well, particularly if each person uses their own bucket and the area is not well fenced to prevent animals from having access to the well.

Dug wells can be improved by using a protected intake. This may use a filter box installed box at the base of the well. Where wells are used, you should ensure that these are covered, have a headwall of at least 30cm above the apron and a handpump or windlass is used.

4.2.4 Rainwater collection

Rainwater collection may be practised by some people and rainwater collection may be promoted as a means to improve water supplies in low-income areas. However, before trying to promote rainwater collection, try to assess how many people already collect rainwater and how many do this in a systematic way using guttering and a tank or drum. Such households may be able to act as promoters of rainwater collection to the rest of their communities. This is the kind of information that you can collect in a water usage study. The climate and in particular rainfall patterns should also be assessed. If rain is infrequent or of overall limited amount, then rainwater collection may not be appropriate.

Where very few people collect rainwater by any means, then promoting rainwater collection may be difficult. It is common that where there is enough rainfall to promote collection, people will already do this even if it is only by placing a bucket under their roof. Where households do not collect rainwater, it suggests that the rainfall is not sufficient for collection or that the population prefers other types of water. Other forms of water supply may be better to promote in such circumstances.

If people do collect rainwater, test the quality of the water and carry out a sanitary inspection. Some of the major problems that you are likely to find are that the roof is dirty and the tank is not cleaned regularly. The roof should be cleaned at the start of every wet season by sweeping the roof and removing any solid material from the gutters. It is also preferred that the collection system has some way of diverting the first flow of water from the roof as this may have picked up excreta from birds and rodents. The household should make sure that the roof is not overhung by trees or close to food stores as this may encourage rodents and lead to excreta on the roof being found.

The tanks should be cleaned at the start of every wet season and the tank should have a drainpipe to allow all the water to be flushed out. If possible, the household should clean the tank by using a dilute chlorine solution. The water from the tank should be drawn from a tap, rather than dipping a bucket into the water as this may cause contamination.

4.2.5 Piped water

Technical interventions for piped water will be undertaken at local (i.e. individual taps or groups of taps) or at larger levels such as supply mains repair. The degree to which surveillance staff will get directly involved in these interventions will depend on how the supply is managed.

Where the piped water is a community-managed supply, it is likely that surveillance staff will become actively involved in the planning and implementation of technical improvements in the same way as for point sources. Where the supply is operated by a separate arm of the local authority or there is a separate water supplier, surveillance staff will involved in identifying problems, making recommendations on actions required and monitoring whether the action has been carried out rather than directly implementing the works.

It is important to assess the sanitary inspection data to identify whether local or major supply faults exist. Where major faults exist, this information should be provided to the water suppliers. Where local problems are found, then these can be included in programmes of support to local communities to reduce risks of contamination.

4.2.6 Local level actions in piped water supplies

Sanitary risks often occur within the environment immediately around the tap. These are problems like the exposure of a pipe close the tap, finding stagnant water close to the tap or the erosion of the area around the tap. In many cases, contamination occurs because of these problems rather than as a result of poor supply management. In these cases, attention should be focused on ensuring that the area around the tap and the customer main is kept clean and that the pipe remains buried.

This is similar in many ways to the issues regarding point sources and also includes some of the health education interventions that are discussed briefly later on. In general, providing advice for the managers of public taps is easier than trying to advise every single household that may have a connection. In any case, the numbers of people using a public tap are likely to be far higher than users of direct household connections.

In many cases, the pipe that connects the tap riser to the supply main is buried at a very shallow depth and therefore is easily exposed and damaged. The particularly weak points are the joints at the connection to the supply main (where pressure may be highest) and the joint between the supply pipe and the riser pipe at the tap itself. In the latter case, this is often damaged when many people use the tap and the riser pipe has no support. Where this is the case, users of the taps should be encouraged to put in a support for the riser pipe. Where there are existing taps, this may have to be a metal support, but for new taps, the use of a concrete plinth should be encouraged.

Communities may sometimes put lengths of hose on the tap to improve the direction of flow of water where the tap design cause a wide stream of water flowing to flow from the tap. These attached pipes may cause contamination and their use should be discouraged. One way to reduce the need for using such attachments is to use taps that have an insert that direct water into a single stream even at high pressure.

An alternative approach is to reduce the distance between the tap outlet and the opening on the water container. The height of the riser pipe can be reduced to a level that is just above he height of the usual container. Riser pipes do not need to be 0.5m high if the usual container is only 0.3m high. Another approach, which may be appropriate when the tap is already in place, is to construct a small plinth to rest the container on that will raise the container up to close to the height of the tap. This will also help to support the tap against damage.

4.2.7 Piped water supply faults

The resolution of supply faults may require either improvement of basic operation and maintenance procedures or significant investment in infrastructure. Using surveillance data to help improve supply in community-managed piped water supplies and in utility supplies is described below.

4.2.7.1 Community-managed supplies

The process of making improvements community-managed piped supplies will be similar to those for point sources. Dialogue with the community, the identification of problems and solutions and development of action plans will all be critical steps in the process. In many community supplies, supply faults relate to deterioration in the source protection measures, similar to those discussed under point sources. These are important to rectify in a community-managed piped water supply.

Other major problems that typically occur relate to the condition of the storage tank(s) and whether the system leaks or often runs below pressure – this could either be daily (related to excess demand) or seasonal due to low flow at the source. By using the sanitary inspection data, the principal shortcomings in the current supply system and what improvements are required, can be identified. In some cases, this will be minor – for instance ensuring that the inspection cover on a storage tank is kept in place or locked. In other cases, more major problems will involve repair of leaks (including possibly replacing broken pipes) or making repairs to the storage tank.

In most cases, it will be expected that the community will have access to available tools and trained staff to undertake simple pipe repairs and repairs to the storage facility. Where these are lacking, a key intervention will be to identify training needs and appropriate people to train from the community. The purchase of tools should, by preference be undertaken by the community, although grants or credit may be available. It would also be expected that some tariff would be levied on these supplies and this would be used to fund operation and maintenance. If these things are not in place, it may be very difficult to sustain community management

4.2.7.2 Utility supplies

Where piped water supplies are provided by a utility, surveillance data should still be used to make improvements, although this will be more likely to entail sharing of information and recommendations and discussions with the utility regarding when they will do the corrective action.

Where water supply services are managed by the local urban authority, the surveillance arm is likely to take a more active role in the resolution of problems. This will include the development of a programme of action to address the problems noted and may include direct participation in some of these activities, such as cleaning of service reservoirs. Where the supply is run by a separate organisation, the actions of the surveillance agency will be more focused on identification and timely reporting of faults and discussion about the implementation of a programme of action.

In both cases, there are basic operation and maintenance activities that should be carried out on a regular basis, which surveillance bodies should monitor. This includes flushing and cleaning of distribution lines and service reservoirs.

Where flushing or cleaning are not regularly carried out, this may become noticeable as colour or odour problems increase or an increased chlorine loss.

4.3 Ensuring good community management

Many interventions will be based on trying to improve community management of water supplies. This may apply to both point sources and public taps. In many cases, water quality failures may have resulted from poor community management and improving capacity at a local level to operate, maintain and manage a water supply is often a major component in water supply improvements. Surveillance data should help to identify major weaknesses in current community-management and allow the surveillance staff to work with communities to strengthen this.

When assessing community management, sanitary inspection data often provides better insights than water quality tests. If the sanitary inspection indicates that risks exist, particularly if these relate to the infrastructure or basic protection measures (for instance fences and ditches) this implies that operation and maintenance is beginning to fail. The greater the number of sanitary risks noted (the overall sanitary risk score) the weaker the operation and maintenance. The quality of water is also likely to deteriorate as the overall sanitary risk score increases.

Using surveillance data, a dialogue can be developed with the community about the quality of their water supply. Using this information, the community and surveillance staff can work towards a consensus about what problems exist, why these problems have arisen and how they can be overcome. In particular this allows a discussion of what actions the community can do themselves and what support they need (technical, training, and financial).

A major issue that should be discussed is whether a water committee exists and whether they are active. It may also be worth reviewing with the community the make-up of the committee and roles and responsibilities of different individuals on the committee. Very often, weaknesses in operation and maintenance result from poor management practices within the community and addressing these may offer significant improvements in the supply. This may implications for training of the committee members.

It is also important to find out whether there is a caretaker for the source. If there is, some basic questions are what work do they currently do and is this effective? If the basic work is not carried out, what are the major problems? Does the caretaker require some payment? In many urban areas, it is less easy to rely on people donating their labour to carry out work and people have limited time. In these cases, it may be easier for community members to provide money to help support operation and maintenance. If this is the case, you will need to spend time with the community to identify how funds can be raised to support a salary for the caretaker and what the relationship of the caretaker should be to the committee. In rural areas, it may be much easier to rely on donation of labour than on payment of a caretaker, but again the actual arrangements put in place should be reviewed.

Each public tap or water source should have a caretaker from the local community who has clearly defined roles and responsibilities. Usually, one caretaker will deal with a single source, but this could be extended to a number of sources in some circumstances. At the back of the manual, are simple checklists for monitoring and operation and maintenance for sources that the caretaker and committee can use to make sure the work required is being carried out. What is important is that the tasks to be completed are reasonable in relation to the remuneration that the caretaker will receive. It should also be stressed, that the community as a whole and the committee in particular also have a responsibility to ensure the water supply remains in good working order and they must ensure that the caretaker has access to the tools and resources needed to maintain the water supply.

Community members can also undertake simple assessment and monitoring of their own water supplies. The checklist in Annex 5 provides a simple system for water source communities and operators to both monitor and maintain sources. If these forms are used, or similar forms are developed for other water supplies, make sure that training is provided to the communities that will use them and make sure that are clear about what information they can collect and how often it is suggested that they collect this information.

4.4 Household water and the safe water chain

Encouraging good handling and storage practices is an important role for health workers and the surveillance data can be very useful in supporting this use the results of tests can be used to demonstrate to people the level of contamination in their drinking water. However, always think carefully about the content of any hygiene advice given and whether the actions being advocated for households are achievable and realistic.

Surveillance information can be used to promote the use of sources that are known to be of good quality. This information can be gained from the routine testing of water. Communicating this information to communities in appropriate ways supports households in making an informed choice about the water source they select. For instance, in one town in Uganda (Soroti), an emphasis was placed on the use of borehole water for drinking as this was the best quality at source found in the town.

The advise on source selection should be supported by information on how this can be protected through good handling and storage practices. The sanitary inspection form for household water quality helps assess whether the storage container is likely to cause contamination of the water. This can be used in developing hygiene education message and in particular to promote the need to keep the inside of the container is clean using either bleach or clean sand. Households should be discouraged from using silt from the area around the water source for cleaning as this often contains contaminated material.

Where the container has a narrow opening (for instance a Jerrycan) then cleaning may be more difficult. The most effective way to clean Jerrycans is to fill it with water and then add some bleach and allow it to stand for at least 30 minutes. Households should rinse the container thoroughly with clean water if this method is followed. The storage container should be cleaned in the same way at least once per week or more often if possible.

Both the container used for collecting water and the one used to store the water in the home, should be covered and the cover only removed when pouring water from the container. It is best for the household to use a container with a tap fitted as this reduces the potential for contamination, as dirty hands cannot enter into the container. If such containers are not available, encourage households to pour water rather than scoop it from the container using a cup as this often leads to contamination when the user has dirty hands.

One particular issue of concern is hygiene education messages focusing on the boiling of drinking water and when such messages are used. In some countries, advice to boil water before drinking is routinely provided to households. Over time, the impact of this message decreases and households stop boiling water because of the cost, taste or because it is perceived as unnecessary.

One consequence of the loss of impact is that there may be increased risks in times of greater urgency for boiling as households feel that the advice is not useful. If the surveillance body wishes to promote boiling as a routine activity, it is important to ensure that this is based on discussions with communities about why it is important for them to continue to boil water even when there appears to be no immediate threat to community health.

4.4.1 Household water treatment

There are several ways, in addition to boiling, by which water may be effectively treated in the home. Where water is clear, chlorine can be added either in the form of tablets in a dilute form of bleach. The free chlorine content of available bleach should be checked before advocating its use to ensure it will be effective.

There are now some specific household treatment units that have been developed which include both a disinfectant and a container with a tap which are often very effective in improving water quality. These are often more effective than adding bleach solutions and are cheaper than boiling water and may be an attractive option for poorer households.

In some areas, households may filter the water either through cloth or by using some form of candle filter. These methods are effective at removing pathogens such as guinea worm but may not reduce contamination from bacteria or viruses. Where candle filters are used, remember that the only types of candle filter that disinfect water are those containing halide resins (for instance iodine). Silver is not a particularly effective disinfectant. Where water is filtered and boiled, you should advise households to filter the water first and then boil it as the candles may support micro-organisms that can enter the water as it passes through the filter. Other local filters may be used, such as a three-pot sand filter which may help reduce the contamination of water but may not remove all the contamination.

4.5 Health and environmental education approaches in communities

The improvements in water sources and water stored within the home that have been described require health and environmental education programmes to be initiated within the community. All interventions to improve water sources or water supplies should be supported by education programmes to help communities sustain source and good hygiene behaviours.

There are many approaches to health education and many methods have been developed and may be appropriate under different circumstances. However, in most cases, people are more likely to make changes in their behaviour and invest time and resources in maintaining a water supply if they have been able to discuss the issues and draw their own conclusions. Participatory methods of education are often the most effective in promoting behaviour change and this may cover a wide variety of aspects including household hygiene practice as well as paying tariffs for water in order to sustain the water supply.

Participatory health and sanitation transformation (PHAST) tools have been used in several countries to promote improvements in water quality. The PHAST approach emphasises the community role in decision-making. Health staff act as facilitators rather than 'teachers' in helping communities understand and discuss problems and identify solutions. It is beyond the scope of this short manual to describe the PHAST methodology in detail, there are other manuals that can be used to help develop these approaches. Usually training should be given to health staff when they undertake PHAST techniques as it is important to understand the purpose and methodology of the approach before trying to use them in the community.

However, the basis of PHAST is that communities and households can and will develop their own solutions to problems. Whilst the PHAST techniques are one particular way of providing the support to this process, participatory methods can be employed without using the specific PHAST tools. At a simple level, the use of community meetings for discussion and problem-solving can be effective in initiating a process of change. If this is supported by water surveillance data then this can be very effective in encouraging community-based solutions to local problems.

Other methods of health education include mass media (such as radio, television and newspapers), drama, song and storytelling as well as delivery of particular messages through meetings and posters. All these methods may have advantages in promoting messages to a large audience, which is obviously not as easy when participatory methods are used.

It is important to be clear as to what you are trying to achieve and what type of message you wish to relay when using these techniques. Avoid making health messages confusing and in particular make sure that they cannot be interpreted in more than one way. For instance, it is often useful to show people both good and bad examples as this often makes the health message clearer.

Make sure that the way in which health education messages are presented is relevant to the target audience. For instance, there may be little point in developing a poster of the benefits of covering a clay storage pot, if everyone uses a Jerrycan to store their water. Always try to pre-test any materials that you use to make sure that your target audience can understand the message that is being presented.

It often helps to present the same message through a variety of different media as this often reinforces an idea in the community. It is also crucial to make the messages interesting and dynamic and therefore it is useful to periodically update or change health messages. When a single type of message is always relayed in the same way, people may start to ignore the message as it is no longer new or interesting.

In all methods of health education, it is often a good idea to focus on the benefits to the community which go beyond health gains. Thus, when trying to promote treatment of water within the home, bringing ideas of better health providing greater opportunities to generate income or enhancing social status is often better than simply emphasising a lack of diarrhoea as a result. Don't forget, many people may not perceive diarrhoea as being more than an inconvenience unless it is severe and life-threatening.

The content of the health messages will depend on the circumstances and therefore there should always be careful consideration of the issues and needs of the communities to be included in hygiene education programmes. Simply adopting materials from elsewhere is rarely appropriate and usually some modification of these materials will be required.

Bear in mind that health education should not just focus on household hygiene and water handling, but also the broader environment. For piped water, it may be important to emphasise the need to pay water bills to avoid disconnection and the need to report major failures in the supply (discontinuity, leaks etc) to the water supplier. The table below provides some ideas about messages you can send using surveillance data.

Focus of activity	Types of message	Surveillance data
Operation and maintenance of a water source	Point sources: maintain protection works; maintain and clear diversion ditches; clear wastewater drains; drain stagnant water; maintain fences. Taps: paying water bills; keeping area around tap clean; reporting faults to the water supplier	Sanitary inspections Water quality results Costs of water and reconnection
Environmental hygiene	Clearing environment of rubbish and faeces; keeping pit latrines away from sources; keeping environment around taps clean	Sanitary inspection data
Promoting safe sources	Use of sources know to be safe for drinking and food preparation	Water quality data
Promoting safe water handling	Using clean containers; using containers with lids	Sanitary inspection data Water quality data
Promoting safe water storage and treatment	Using clean containers; using containers with lids, pouring or using a tap to get water; treatment of water	Sanitary inspection data Water quality data

Table 3: Health education message using surveillance data

It is also a good idea to build capacity within the community to monitor their water source and water handling practices. This can help the community develop their own mechanisms for ongoing sustained good operation and maintenance of the source and good hygiene practices within the home. The simple checklists at the end of manual provide one way of helping communities to monitor their own water sources. However, bear in mind that communities may have their own priorities concerning water and you may need to adapt the checklists to ensure that the approach is relevant to the needs of the community. When encouraging communities to monitor their water supply, it is important that the information generated by the community can be linked to the information generated through surveillance. Otherwise, a situation will result where one set of information is disregarded and this may limit the effectiveness of interventions.

Identifying people within the community who can acts as local health promoters is often a good way for encouraging ongoing efforts to improve health within communities. This may take time to establish and there should be a commitment from the community to support such activities. These people can act as the main conduits for information regarding water quality and supply that you have collected through your routine activities and will become a focal point for improved environmental health within their community.

Annexes

Annex 1: Inventory Form

Urban and Peri-Urban Water Supply Surveillance Project, EHD, Ministry of Health

Inventory observation sheet and questionnaire

Water source No. [ ]

Name of water source	[ ]
Location	[ ]
Parish	[ ]
Division	[ ]
Town	[ ]
Interviewer's name	[ ]
Date	[ ]

1 What is the water source:
Tick 1 box

Public standpost	[ ]
Private tapstand - water selling	[ ]
Landlord provided tap	[ ]
Protected spring in good condition	[ ]
Protected spring requiring repair	[ ]
Unprotected spring	[ ]
Borehole with handpump	[ ]
Dug well with no handpump/windlass	[ ]
Dug well with windlass	[ ]
Dug well with handpump	[ ]
Rooftop rainwater catchment	[ ]
Unprotected scoop well	[ ]
Pond/stream/swamp/lake	[ ]

If the source is a pond, stream, swamp, lake, unprotected spring or unprotected scoop well, only answer questions 1-5 and 14-22

2 Who owns the water source:
Tick 1 box

Private owner	[ ]
NWSC	[ ]
Community	[ ]
Local Councils (LCI/II)	[ ]
City/Town Councils (LCIII-V)	[ ]
Project	[_____] [ ]
No-one	[ ]

3 Who supervises the water supply
Tick 1 box

Owner	[ ]
Community caretaker	[ ]
Other community representative	[ ]
Project staff	[ ]
Other	[_____] [ ]
No-one	[ ]

4 Is the water provided:
Tick 1 box

Free of charge	[ ]
Cost per bucket/jerry can	[ ]
Meter/flat rate	[ ]

If water is free go to question 6

5 How much is charged for the water   USh [   ] per [   ]
   Get information from source caretaker USh [   ] per [   ]

6 Who did the actual construction of the
   water supply
   Tick one box - get information from source
   caretaker or from your records

Community	[ ]
NGO/Donor	[ ]
Contractor	[ ]
Govt agency	[ ]
Other (who)	[ ]
City/Town/District council (LCIII-V)	[ ]

7 Which Project/Organisation sponsored
   the design and construction
   Get information from source caretaker or from
   your records

[   ]

8 When was it constructed
   Tick one box - get information from source
   caretaker or from your records

0-6 months	[ ]
6-12 months	[ ]
More than 1 year	[ ]
Don't know/don't remember	[ ]

9 Has any repair or rehabilitation work
   been carried out on the water supply
   Tick one box - get information from
   source caretaker

Yes	[ ]
No	[ ]

If 'no' go to question 14

10 What was the most recent repair
    Get information from source caretaker

[   ]

11 Who did this
    If more than one organisation tick all the
    appropriate boxes

Community	
City/Town/District Council (LCIII-V)	
Govt Agency	[ ]
NGO/Donor	[ ]
Owner	

12 When was it done
    Tick one box - get information from
    source caretaker

0-6 months	[ ]
6-12 months	[ ]
More than 1 year	[ ]
Don't know/remember	[ ]

13 Who paid for the work to be done
If more than one organisation tick all the
appropriate boxes

Community
City/Town Council (LCIII-V)
Govt Agency
NGO/Donor
Owner

14 Who is responsible for maintenance of
the source
If more than one organisation tick all the
appropriate boxes

Community
City/Town Council (LCIII-V)
Govt Agency
NGO/Donor
Owner
Don't know
No-one
If 'don't know' or 'no-one' go to question 17

15 Who pays for maintenance work
If more than one organisation tick all the
appropriate boxes

Community
City/Town Council (LCIII-V)
Govt Agency
NGO/Donor
Owner
Don't know
No-one

16 How often is this done
Tick one box - get information from
source caretaker

Daily
More than once a week
Weekly
More than once a month
Monthly
Less than once a month
Don't know

17 Who is responsible for cleaning the area
around the source
If more than one organisation tick all the
appropriate boxes

Community
City/Town Council (LCIII-V)
Govt Agency
NGO/Donor
Owner
No-one
Don't know
If no-one go to question 19

18 How often is this done
Tick one box - get information from
source caretaker

Daily
More than once a week
Weekly
More than once a month
Monthly
Less than once a month
Don't know

19 Do you restrict how much water each   Yes
    person can take   No
                                             If 'no' go to question 21

Tick one box - get information from source caretaker. NB: does not include restriction because of lack of n

20 Why is there a restriction   Source has low flow
    Tick one box - get information from   Too many people use source
    source caretaker   Limited time for caretaker
                                             Non-domestic uses of water
                                             Other (specify)
                                             Don't know

21 Does the source dry up   Yes
                                             No
                                             If 'yes' answer question 22

Tick one box - get information from source caretaker. NB: does not include disconnection)

22 If the source does dry up, does this happen   Daily
    Tick one box - get information from   Monthly
    source caretaker   Seasonally
                                                   Occassionally

Annex 2: Daily Report Sheet

Daily Report Sheet

Town/City

Analyst

mple source	Source code No.	SI score	Time	Colour	Turbidity TU	Chlorine		pH	Thermotolerant c	
						Free	Total		Vol ml.	No. colonies

s

of analyst

Annex 3: Sanitary Inspection Forms

I.   **Type of Facility**   **PIPED WATER**

1.   General Information :   Division:

:   Parish

2.   Code Number

3.   Date of Visit

4.   Water samples taken? ……..   Sample Nos. ………

II   **Specific Diagnostic Information for Assessment**

	Risk	**Sample No**
(please indicate at which sample sites the risk was identified)		
1. Do any tapstands leak	Y/N	…………..
2. Does surface water collect around any tapstand?	Y/N	…………..
3. Is the area uphill of any tapstand eroded?	Y/N	…………..
4. Are pipes exposed close to any tapstand?	Y/N	…………..
5. Is human excreta on the ground within 10m of any tapstand?	Y/N	…………..
6. Is there a sewer within 30m of any tapstand?	Y/N	…………..
7. Has there been discontinuity in the last 10 days at any tapstand?	Y/N	…………..
8. Are there signs of leaks in the mains pipes in the Parish?	Y/N	…………..
9. Do the community report any pipe breaks in the last week?	Y/N	…………..
10. Is the main pipe exposed anywhere in the Parish?	Y/N	…………..

Total Score of Risks   …./10

Risk score: 9-10 = Very high; 6-8 = High; 3-5 = Medium; 0-3 = Low

III   Results and Recommendations:
The following important points of risk were noted: (list nos. 1-10)

Signature of Health Inspector/Assistant:

Comments:

I.   **Type of Facility**   **PIPED WATER WITH SERVICE RESERVOIR**

1.   General Information   :   Zone

                             :   Town

2.   Code Number

3.   Date of Visit

4.   Water samples taken? ……..   Sample Nos. ………

II   **Specific Diagnostic Information for Assessment**

(please indicate at which sample sites the risk was identified)

	Risk	Sample No
1. Do any standpipes leak at sample sites?	Y/N	………….
2. Does water collect around any sample site?	Y/N	………….
3. Is area uphill eroded at any sample site?	Y/N	………….
4. Are pipes exposed close to any sample site?	Y/N	………….
5. Is human excreta on ground within 10m of standpipe?	Y/N	………….
6. Sewer or latrine within 30m of sample site?	Y/N	………….
7. Has there been discontinuity within last 10 days at sample site?	Y/N	………….
8. Are there signs of leaks in sampling area?	Y/N	………….
9. Do users report pipe breaks in last week?	Y/N	………….
10. Is the supply main exposed in sampling area?	Y/N	………….
11. Is the service reservoir cracked or leaking?	Y/N	………….
12. Are the air vents or inspection cover insanitary?	Y/N	………….

                         Total Score of Risks   …./10

Risk score: 10-12 = Very high; 8-10 = High; 5-7 = Medium; 2-4 = Low; 0-1 = Very Low

III   **Results and Recommendations:**

The following important points of risk were noted: (list nos. 1-12)

Signature of Health Inspector/Assistant:

Comments:

I.   **Type of Facility**   **GRAVITY-FED PIPED WATER**

1.   General Information :   System name:

2.   Code Number

3.   Date of Visit

4.   Water samples taken? ……..   Sample Nos. ………

II   **Specific Diagnostic Information for Assessment**

	Risk	**Sample No**
(please indicate at which sample sites the risk was identified)		
1. Does the pipe leak between the source and storage tank?	Y/N	
2. Is the storage tank cracked, damaged or leak?	Y/N	
3. Are the vents and covers on the tank damaged or open?	Y/N	
4. Do any tapstands leak?	Y/N	………….
5. Does surface water collect around any tapstand?	Y/N	………….
6. Is the area uphill of any tapstand eroded?	Y/N	………….
7. Are pipes exposed close to any tapstand?	Y/N	…………
8. Is human excreta on the ground within 10m of any tapstand?	Y/N	………….
9. Has there been discontinuity n the last 10 days at any tapstand?	Y/N	………….
10. Are there signs of leaks in the main supply pipe in the system?	Y/N	………….
11. Do the community report any pipe breaks in the last week?	Y/N	………….
12. Is the main supply pipe exposed anywhere in the system?	Y/N	………….

Total Score of Risks   …./12

Risk score: 10-12 = Very high; 8-10 = High; 5-7 = Medium; 2-4 = Low; 0-1 = Very Low

III   **Results and Recommendations:**
The following important points of risk were noted: (list nos. 1-12)

Signature of Health Inspector/Assistant:

Comments:

I.   **Type of Facility**   **BOREHOLE WITH HANDPUMP**

1.   General Information   :   Division:

                                :   Parish

2.   Code Number

3.   Date of Visit

4.   Water sample taken? ……..   Sample No. ……… TTC/100ml ………..

II   <u>**Specific Diagnostic Information for Assessment**</u>

                                                                       Risk

1. Is there a latrine within 10m of the borehole?   Y/N

2. Is there a latrine uphill of the borehole?   Y/N

3. Are there any other sources of pollution within 10m of borehole?   Y/N
       (e.g. animal breeding, cultivation, roads, industry etc)

4. Is the drainage faulty allowing ponding within 2m of the borehole?   Y/N

5. Is the drainage channel cracked, broken or need cleaning?   Y/N

6. Is the fence missing or faulty?   Y/N

7. Is the apron less than 1m in radius?   Y/N

8. Does spilt water collect in the apron area?   Y/N

9. Is the apron cracked or damaged?   Y/N

10. Is the handpump loose at the point of attachment to apron?   Y/N

                                      Total Score of Risks   …./10
Risk score: 9-10 = Very high; 6-8 = High; 3-5 = Medium; 0-3 = Low

III   **Results and Recommendations:**
The following important points of risk were noted: (list nos. 1-10)

Signature of Health Inspector/Assistant:

Comments:

I.   **Type of Facility**   **PROTECTED SPRING**

1.   General Information :   Division:

                           :   Parish

2.   Code Number:

3.   Date of Visit:

4.   Water sample taken? ....   Sample No. .... TTC/100ml ....

II   **Specific Diagnostic Information for Assessment**

                                                                  Risk

1. Is the spring unprotected?   Y/N

2. Is the masonry protecting the spring faulty?   Y/N

3. Is the backfill area behind the retaining wall eroded?   Y/N

4. Does spilt water flood the collection area?   Y/N

5. Is the fence absent or faulty?   Y/N

6. Can animals have access within 10m of the spring?   Y/N

7. Is there a latrine uphill and/or within 30m of the spring?   Y/N

8. Does surface water collect uphill of the spring?   Y/N

9. Is the diversion ditch above the spring absent or non-functional?   Y/N

10. Are there any other sources of pollution uphill of the spring?   Y/N
    (e.g. solid waste)
                            Total Score of Risks   ..../10

Risk score: 9-10 = Very high; 6-8 = High; 3-5 = Medium; 0-3 = Low

III   **Results and Recommendations:**
The following important points of risk were noted: (list nos. 1-10)

Signature of Health Inspector/Assistant:

Comments:

I. Type of Facility   DUG WELL WITH HANDPUMP/WINDLASS

1. General Information   :   Division:

                          :   Parish

2. Code Number

3. Date of Visit

4. Water sample taken? ……..   Sample No. ……… TTC/100ml ………..

II   Specific Diagnostic Information for Assessment

	Risk
1. Is there a latrine within 10m of the well?	Y/N
2. Is the nearest latrine uphill of the well?	Y/N
3. Is there any other source of pollution within 10m of well? (e.g. animal breeding, cultivation, roads, industry etc)	Y/N
4. Is the drainage faulty allowing ponding within 2m of the well?	Y/N
5. Is the drainage channel cracked, broken or need cleaning?	Y/N
6. Is the fence missing or faulty?	Y/N
7. Is the cement less than 1m in radius around the top of the well?	Y/N
8. Does spilt water collect in the apron area?	Y/N
9. Are there cracks in the cement floor?	Y/N
10. Is the handpump loose at the point of attachment to well head?	Y/N
11. Is the well-cover insanity?	Y/N
Total Score of Risks	…./11

Risk score: 9-11 = Very high; 6-8 = High; 3-5 = Medium; 0-3 = Low

III   Results and Recommendations:

The following important points of risk were noted: (list nos. 1-11)

Signature of Health Inspector/Assistant:

Comments:

I. Type of Facility   RAINWATER COLLECTION AND STORAGE

1. General Information : Division:

    : Parish

2. Code Number

3. Date of Visit

4. Water sample taken? ……..   Sample No. ……… TTC/100ml ………..

II   Specific Diagnostic Information for Assessment

	Risk
1. Is rainwater collected in an open container?	Y/N
2. Are there visible signs of contamination on the roof catchment? (e.g. plants, excreta, dust)	Y/N
3. Is guttering that collects water dirty or blocked?	Y/N
4. Are the top or walls of the tank cracked or damaged?	Y/N
5. Is water collected directly from the tank (no tap on the tank)?	Y/N
6. Is there a bucket in use and is this left where it can become contaminated?	Y/N
7. Is the tap leaking or damaged?	Y/N
8. Is the concrete floor under the tap defective or dirty?	Y/N
9. Is there any source of pollution around the tank or water collection area?	Y/N
10. Is the tank clean inside?	Y/N
Total Score of Risks	…./10

Risk score: 9-10 = Very high; 6-8 = High; 3-5 = Medium; 0-3 = Low

III   Results and Recommendations:
The following important points of risk were noted: (list nos. 1-10)

Signature of Health Inspector/Assistant:

Comments:

Household water quality inspection

1.   Is drinking water kept in a separate container (ask to be shown this)?

☐ Yes   ☐ No

2.   Is drinking water container kept above floor level and away from contamination?

☐ Yes   ☐ No

3.   Do water containers have a narrow mouth/opening?

☐ Yes   ☐ No

4.   Do containers have a lid/cover?

☐ Yes   ☐ No

5.   Is this is in place at time of visit

☐ Yes   ☐ No

6.   How is water taken from the container?

☐ Poured   ☐ Cup   ☐ Other utensil

7.   Is the utensil used to draw water from the container clean?

☐ Yes   ☐ No

8.   Is the utensil used to draw water the container kept away from surfaces and stored in a hygienic manner?

☐ Yes   ☐ No

9.   How often is the container cleaned?

☐ Every day   ☐ Every month   ☐ Never

☐ Every week   ☐ Rarely

10.   How is the container cleaned?

....

11.   Is the inside of the drinking water container clean?

☐ Yes   ☐ No

12.   Is the outside of the drinking container clean?

☐ Yes   ☐ No

Annex 4: Community Feedback Forms

Urban and Peri-Urban Water Supply Surveillance Project

Area:

…e Public Health Department recently came to your community and took water quality samples and carried out sanitary insp…
…below. The results of the survey are shown in the table.

	Source type	Faecal contamination	Sanitary risk score	Major risk points noted	State of water sourc…
		Yes No			

…ontamination is yes, this means your water is contaminated with excreta and is a risk to the health of those who drink this …
…sk score shows the level of risk of contamination in your supply.
…s noted show the major problems with your water supply.

…ng recommendations are made for your community on the basis of the above results:

Urban and Peri-Urban Water Supply Surveillance Project

Area:

Public Health Department recently came to your community and took water quality samples and carried out sanitary inspec[...] [l]ow. The results of the survey are shown in the table.

Source type	Faecal contamination	Sanitary risk score	Major risk points noted	State of water source
	None Low Medium Severe	Low Medium High		

[...]faecal contamination shows you how contaminated your water source is. Higher levels of contamination represent increas[...] [he]alth.
[...] score shows the level of risk of contamination in your supply.
[...] [n]oted show the major problems with your water supply.

[... r]ecommendations are made for your community on the basis of the above results:

Annex 5: Community Monitoring and Maintenance Forms

Community checklist for monitoring a protected spring

Checklist	No	Yes	Action
Does the water in the spring change colour after heavy rain?			
Have the public health department from KCC tested your spring recently?			
Were you told the result and given any advice?			
Did you act on the advice?			
Is the retaining wall showing any signs of damage?			
Does the retaining wall need repair – what is this and can you do it yourself?			
If you cannot do it, is there anyone in your community who can do this repair?			
How much will the repair cost? (think about labour as well as material)			
Does the uphill diversion ditch need cleaning?			
When was it last cleaned?			
Is the drainage ditch below the spring blocked or need clearing?			
Does the fence need any repairs?			
If repairs are need, what is required and can you do it yourself?			
If you cannot do it, is there anyone in your community who can do this repair?			
How much will the repair cost? (think about labour as well as material)			

Checklist	No	Yes	Action
Do the steps need cleaning?			
Do the steps need any repair?			
If repairs are need, what is required and can you do it yourself?			
If you cannot do it, is there anyone in your community who can do this repair?			
If there is a hedge, does this need trimming?			
When was the hedge last trimmed?			
Does the grass within the fence need slashing?			
When did you last slash the grass?			
Are the outlets from the retaining wall showing any leaks?			
Are there any other problems with your spring that need attention?			
What are these?			

Operator activity sheet for maintenance of a protected spring

Activity	Dry season	Wet season	
		Routine	**After heavy rainfall**
Clear uphill diversion ditch	At least once per month	At least once per week	Clean if required
Clear drainage ditch from outlets	At least once per month	At least once per week	Clean if required
Slashing grass inside fence	At least once per dry season	At least once per month	Not necessary
Make sure steps are clean and not broken	At least once per week	At least once per week	Clean if required
Clear rubbish away from area around spring, particularly uphill	At least once per week	At least once per week	Clean if required
Keep paths and grassed areas above springs clear of rubbish	At least once per month	At least once per month	
Trim hedge once it reaches a height of 4 feet	Do not trim in the dry season	As soon as hedge reaches 4 feet in height	Not necessary
Carry out regular inspections of the spring and note any faults	At least twice per week	Daily	After every heavy rains

www.ingramcontent.com/pod-product-compliance
Lightning Source LLC
Chambersburg PA
CBHW080628030426
42336CB00018B/3117